Boomerang Adventures

How India is embracing this unique sport

Daniel Joshua

SPI PUBLICATIONS

Published by SPI Publications, www.spipublications.in
SPI, the SPI logo, and Split Poetry India are trademarks of SPI Publications, or its affiliates.
ISBN-13: 978-93-49860-50-6

First Edition 2025

SPI Publications

Corporate & Editorial Office
117/2, Sector 37, Khandsa Road,
Gurgaon, Haryana 122 001
Phone: +91 98355 52940
Email: contact@spipublications.in
Website: www.spipublications.in

Processed and Printed in India

TABLE OF CONTENT

Daniel's Boomerang

Throw it to Know it

Designed and conceptualized by -
Daniel Joshua, India

Proof read by -
Gary Broadbent, U. S. A

Broadbent Boomerangs
Boomerangs are coming back!

Sponsored by -
Oscar Cuartas Boomerang Foundation, U.S

Oscar Cuartas Boomerang Foundation

WELCOME MESSAGE

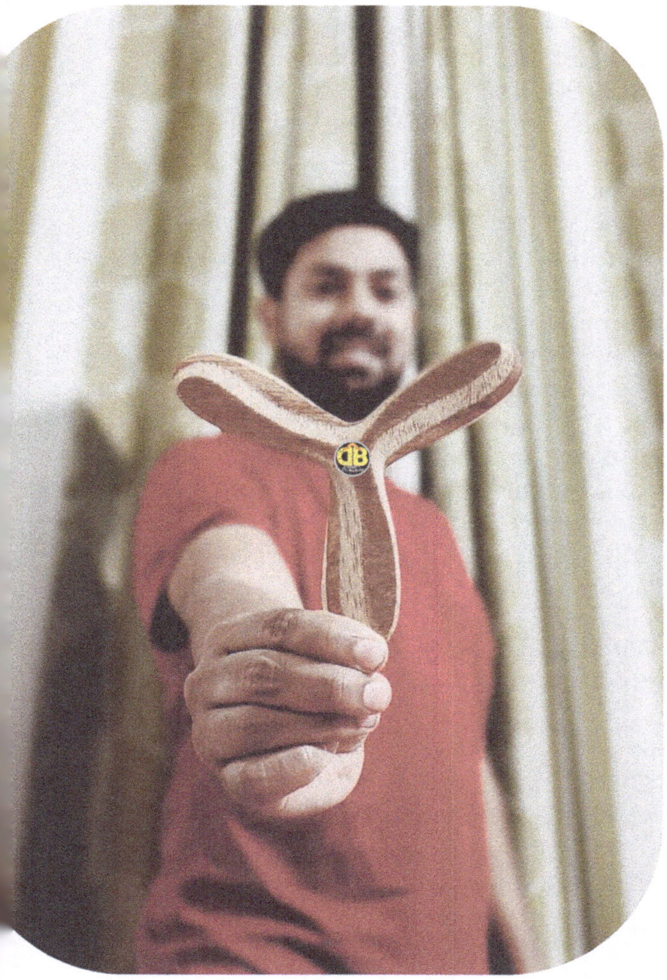

Greetings and welcome to 'Daniel's Boomerang.' For many months our team has been traveling across the country with the sole aim of bringing awareness of Sport Boomerang Throwing.

If you don't know Sport Boomerang Throwing, it's a unique sport that's been played in many countries for many decades. Boomerangs are unique because they magically return to the thrower after being thrown the right way.

Historically, the indigenous people used throwsticks or a Kylie for hunting purposes. Unlike boomerang those were deadly and wouldn't return back to the thrower.
Modern sport boomerangs are usually made from various fibres, plastics, plywoods, hardwoods and most are very light weighted.

At Daniel's Boomerang, we are dedicated to providing quality boomerangs to both new throwers and pro throwers. At our academy, we train throwers and help them prepare for both, serious competitions as well as healthy and fun mind and body exercise.
From time to time we organise workshops to promote the sport in India and our neighboring country, Nepal.
So far we have gifted more than 300 boomerangs during our awareness programs.
Professional handmade boomerangs are available for very reasonable prices at our store.

I invite and encourage you to try your hand at this new, budding sport in India. All you gotta do is...
Throw It -- To Know It

DANIEL JOSHUA
FOUNDER
DANIEL'S BOOMERANG

ANCIENT HISTORY

Boomerangs came in the Dreamtime, or the beginning of the world, according to Australian Aboriginal legends. It is believed that the first boomerangs created geographical features across the continent. Stories about Central Australia's enormous monolith Uluru, the coloured beach sands of Queensland's Sunshine Coast, and Constellation Scorpius in the night sky, all include boomerangs.

Aboriginal Rock Art is painted, engraved and stenciled on stone surfaces, and in the Kimberley region of Western Australia boomerangs in hunting scenes are about 20,000 years old. And in Arnhem Land, Northern Territory the oldest images of boomerangs were painted about 25,000 years ago.

Although a famous Australian object and symbol, boomerang-like implements have been discovered in Africa, Europe, India, and North and South America. They include wooden weapons excavated in Denmark and the Netherlands, and non-return throw-sticks used by the Hopi natives of Arizona to hunt rabbits. An outstanding artefact unearthed in Oblazowa Cave in Poland was shaped from a mammoth's tusk about 30,000 years ago. Yet the most surprising are "boomerangs" discovered in Tutankhamun's tomb in Egypt. Several are made from ivory with gold tips, and modern wooden replicas demonstrate that some of these 3,300 year old artefacts can fly and return!

Traditional Aboriginal returning (come-back) boomerangs, carved in many shapes and sizes, were rarely if ever decorated, but non-returning (straight-flying) boomerangs were finely grooved, engraved or painted with ochres. Tribal men threw returners in games and as flying decoys to hunt ducks and waterfowl. Non-returners were multi-purpose tools for hunting, fighting and ceremony, and also percussion instruments in dance and storytelling.

A rare and exciting discovery of boomerangs was made at Wyrie Swamp in South Australia in 1973. Amazingly preserved in a peat bog for about 10,000 years, they are the oldest wooden boomerangs ever found!

Modern boomerangs are linked through time to ancient Aboriginal boomerangs and the oldest continuous culture on earth. That is why boomerang throwing is called the "world's oldest sport!"

Ancient boomerangs. Source - National geographic

Aboriginal man with boomerang

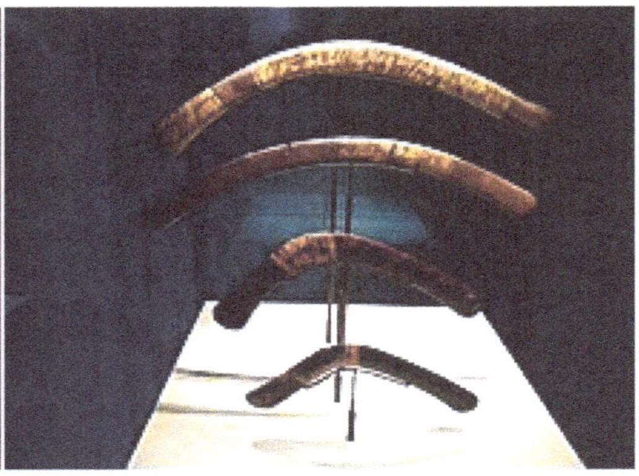

4 boomerangs of the tomb of pharaoh Tutankhamun (1336-1326 BC)

Early discoveries indicate how our ancestors in the southern region of India, particularly in Tamil Nadu, used these objects for hunting and referred to them as 'Valaris'. I am proud to mention that Mr. Philip Sathyaraj from Tamil Nadu, a friend who shares my passion for boomerangs, gifted one of his handmade Valaris to Gunter Möller, Former President of the 'International Federation of Boomerang Associations', as a souvenir during his participation in the World Boomerang Championship, 2022 in France. This act highlights the significance of boomerangs in Indian culture.
Are you ready to be a part of it? #ThrowItToKnowIt

THE EVOLUTION OF COMPETITIVE SPORT

During the dynamic era of the 1970s and 1980s, a group of pioneering figures stood out as key influencers in the world of boomerang crafting and competitive sports. Among them were Herb Smith from the UK, Ben Ruhe, Al Gerhards, and Ted Bailey from the USA, and Oscar Cuartas from Colombia. These innovators boldly ventured beyond the confines of traditional aboriginal boomerang shapes, delving into experiments with different models, shapes, and weights to push the boundaries of the craft.

Oscar Cuartas, known for his inventive spirit and exquisite craftmanship, took boomerang design to new heights by incorporating techniques of craftmanship from his experience making musical instruments into boomerang making. Oscar blended perfectly blended feather lapped layers of wood venneers, lap joints, aluminum inner cores and thinly sliced strip laminated elbows, and introduced golf ball dimples on the surface of boomerangs. This groundbreaking approach aimed to reduce drag and enhance flight distance, showcasing a blend of creativity and scientific insight.

Ben Ruhe, along with the Rufh brothers, Peter and Larry, played a vital role in the revival of the sport in America and in establishing the rules and modalities that govern modern competitive boomerang sports. Their collaborative efforts not only standardized the sport but also paved the way for the World Boomerang Championships and the sport global recognition and participation.

The relentless curiosity and dedication of these trailblazers revitalized boomerang crafting and competitive sports, bridging the ancient art form with contemporary innovations. Their legacy continues to inspire enthusiasts worldwide, shaping the ongoing evolution and popularity of boomerang culture.

Master Oscar Cuartas, Colombia

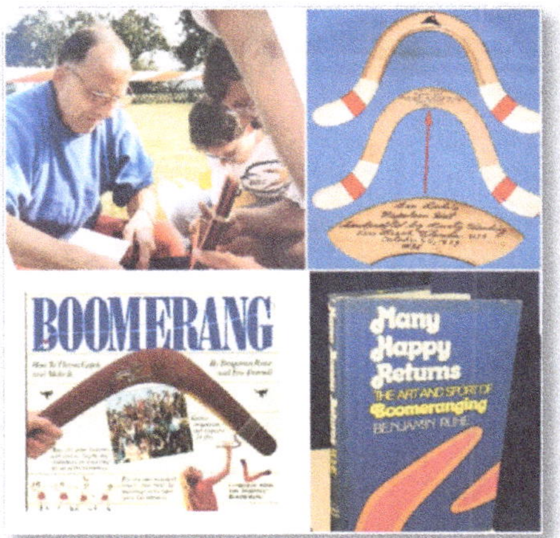

Master Benjamin Ruhe, U.S.A

Master Herb Smith, U.K

BOOMERANG SPORT

An In-Depth Look at the Various Rounds

Every 2 years a World Boomerang Championship (WBC) is celebrated with the following categories -

Accuracy Round : In the Accuracy round, participants throw their boomerangs from a bullseye marked on the ground. Points are awarded based on the proximity of the boomerang to the bullseye. It's a true test of precision and control.

Trick Catch : The Trick Catch round adds a touch of flair to the competition. Throwers perform a variety of catches, including one-handed catches with both the left and right hand, behind-the-back catches, under-the-leg catches, and more. The challenge intensifies when attempting these catches with two boomerangs simultaneously.

Fast Catch : As the name suggests, the Fast Catch round revolves around speed. Competitors aim to make five throws and catches as quickly as possible, racing against the clock for victory.

Endurance : Endurance ups the stakes by challenging participants to engage in Fast Catch for a relentless five-minute duration. The individual with the highest number of successful catches within the time limit emerges as the victor.

Maximum Time Aloft (MTA) : MTA is all about achieving the longest airtime for the boomerang before catching it. This round utilizes specialized MTA boomerangs, presenting a fascinating display of flight and control.

Australian Round : Combining distance, accuracy, and catching prowess, the Australian Round demands a multi-faceted approach. Participants aim for maximum distance with a 50-meter range boomerang while prioritizing bullseye catches for accuracy and points.

Long Distance : In the Long Distance event, participants strive to achieve impressive boomerang flight distances. The current world record stands at an astounding 238 meters, providing a glimpse of the exceptional skill and power involved in this round.

It's important to note that all boomerangs must meet a minimum range requirement of 20 meters, as judged by range officials positioned throughout the field. Bonus points are awarded in the Aussie Round for exceeding the 30-meter mark.

Aesthetic Competition : This competition in Boomerang Sport showcases the artistic side of boomerangs, judged on craftsmanship, natural shape, decoration, related objects, throwsticks, and overall appeal. It highlights creativity and attention to detail, allowing participants to display their skills and passion for boomerang design.

Boomerang sport encompasses a captivating blend of skill, precision, speed, and endurance, making it an enthralling experience for competitors and spectators alike. These rounds showcase the exciting and diverse nature of this extraordinary sport.

The World Boomerang Championship, organized by the IFBA (International Federation of Boomerang Associations), is overseen by its current President, **Mr. Logan Broadbent**, who is also a world champion.

FREQUENTLY ASKED QUESTIONS

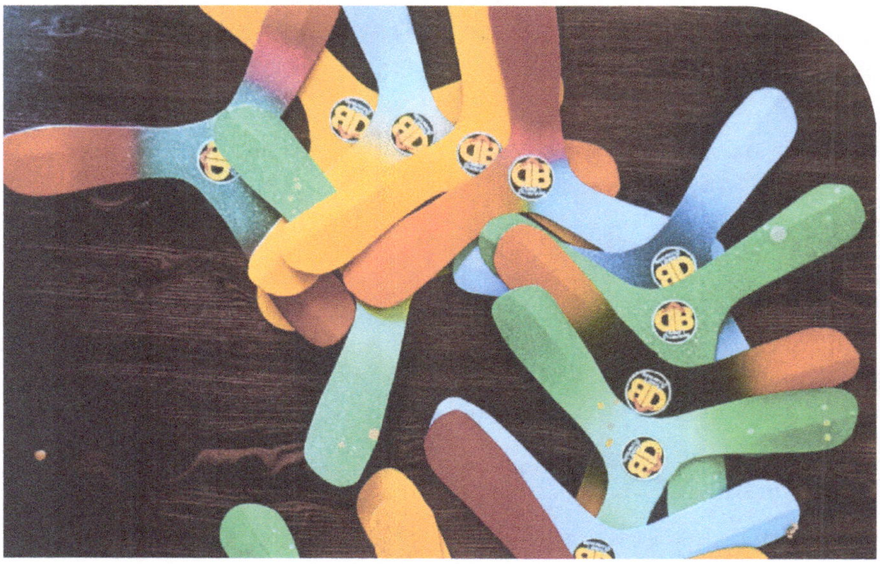

What is a boomerang?
Boomerang is an interesting sport that requires practice, skill and focus. It is a sport that has been around for centuries and is played in many countries around the world. It involves throwing a curved, flat object (boomerang) in a particular direction, and then having it return to the thrower. The 'Jungle Book' character 'Mowgli' used to have a curved piece of wood, popularly known as 'Mowgli ka panja', which was a traditional shaped boomerang.

What is it made up of?
The boomerang is typically made of wood, plastic, fiberglass, carbon fiber, paper, etc and the best makers use a combination of materials to ensure the most successful throws and catch. Experienced boomerang makers keep experimenting with new materials to make boomerangs.

How does it function? / Why does it return back to the thrower?
The science behind boomerang throwing is quite complex and involves understanding the principles of aerodynamics, Bernoulli's principle, gyroscopic precession gravity, and Newton's laws of motion. The way a boomerang is thrown, and the angle of the curve, affects how far it can fly and how quickly it returns.
A professional boomerang thrower also knows how to tune his boomerang to make it fly higher or lower, farther or closer and to make its return perfect.

Who are some of the best current boomerang throwers in the world?

Some of the best current boomerang throwers in the world include Logan Broadbent, Richard and Daniel Bower from the USA, Manuel Schutz from Switzerland, Fridolin Frost from Germany, Andre Caixeta and Eduardo Mistico from Brazil, Denis Suprana from Indonesia, Grant Perry from Australia, and Sunil Uikey from India, etc.

Can I learn/throw a boomerang?

Boomerang is a great sport for anyone who is looking for some outdoor fun. It can also be a great way to get some exercise and practice hand-eye coordination. There are many records kept for boomerang throwing, such as the longest throw and most late landing (MTA which means Maximum Time Aloft).

If you're looking for a new sport to try, boomerang could be the perfect choice. It's fun, challenging and a great way to pass the time. With a bit of practice and dedication, you could even start competing in boomerang tournaments. So, why not give it a go?

What are the different categories in boomerang sport?

Some of the main categories are Fast catch, Endurance, Accuracy, MTA, Aussie, Trick Catch, Team event, Long Distance (LD) and Throwstick (non-returning boomerang).

What shapes and sizes are boomerangs available in?

Traditional boomerangs, including many other modern boomerangs are available in 'V' or 'U' shape (two wings). Three winged boomerangs are the most commonly seen modern boomerang shapes, however four blader, five blader, six blader and even fancy, decorative, theme-based boomerang designs can be seen used by many professional throwers as per their own choice.

I and Philip Sathyaraj (India), Koko Handoko (Indonesia), Collin De Graag (Europe), Adhit (Indonesia) and many other boomerang makers from other countries are some who keep experimenting with making new designs, decorations and models of boomerangs.

Where can I get boomerangs from?

You can buy low-priced boomerangs made by Daniel's Boomerang by contacting us, where a professional boomerang expert will be able to help you choose from a wide range of boomerangs, so you don't end up buying just something which you might not be able to eventually use.

You can also buy imported boomerangs made by renowned boomerang makers from around the world that are available for purchase at Daniel's Boomerang or directly by them.

Boomerangs from other countries can be made available too, on demand.

Do I need to be a professional thrower to be able to participate in events organized by Daniel's Boomerang?

At Daniel's Boomerang, we recognize that simply considering participation in a boomerang event demonstrates a level of dedication and enthusiasm worthy of recognition. We acknowledge that every expert begins with fundamental skills, and continuous learning is a shared journey. Therefore, we invite you to join us on the field, where collective practice and shared knowledge foster growth and improvement. Embrace the journey, and let's advance together.

VISION & MISSION

Workshops & Awareness Programs

We have so far conducted more than 30 workshops in schools, colleges, slums, orphanages, villages, streets and amongst working professionals. Through these workshops, we have been able to bring awareness to the Boomerang sport among not less than 5000 people with at least a hundred new throwers added to the Indian throwers community.

Competitions, Events and Tournaments

With the number of new throwers continuously being added to the list of the Indian Boomerang community through our workshops and awareness programs, various tournaments and competitions are organized to encourage and make them ready for the other boomerang championships.

Laser cutting a self concept design by Daniel Joshua

Boomerang Making

Boomerangs aren't 'easy to get' things in India. Other than that, it isn't very cheap either, because India is very new to this sport and therefore most boomerangs makers are from Australia, Europe, U. K and America. Importing costs much.

At Daniel's Boomerang, we make boomerangs that comply with international standards, we also make short-range beginner boomerangs for really cheap prices.

TEAM, PARTNERS & FRIENDS

RAJAN B. SAFRI, U. S - MASTER CHEF & PARTNER D. B

The first time I saw Daniel throwing boomerangs and catching them back, I was amazed to see how it flies so far but then returns perfectly to the very place it started from. I immediately took an interest in it and wanted to try it myself. And here we are I am a proud partner of Daniel's Boomerang and look forward to working with the team. I also loved the 'Customized Memento' that was presented to me.

SUNIL UIKEY, BOOMERANG THROWER - MADHYA PRADESH PARTICIPATED IN WORLD BOOMERANG CHAMPIONSHIP 2022 BORDEAUX FRANCE

Boomerang for me is LIFE and I'm so glad to be associated with 'Daniel's Boomerang' especially because of the dedication I get to see in the team.

Throwers registered under this banner are wonder makers, including the junior category. I am glad to have been able to guide and teach some of them, especially to see them learning & performing so quickly.

In terms of being associated with this sport, I'm Daniel's senior but I can proudly say that I am enjoying a lot being associated with him.

PHILIP SATHYARAJ, BOOMERANG MAKER & EXPERT - TN PARTICIPATED IN WORLD BOOMERANG CHAMPIONSHIP 2022 BORDEAUX FRANCE

I met Danny in May 2022 in a tournament that he was hosting. He was very passionate about the sport. I showed him some of the boomerangs made by me. I asked him to try making his boomerangs because that is the fastest way to learn the sport. He obliged and started making his own. Now he has his brand of boomerangs. Danny is doing a great job by introducing the sport all over north India in schools and colleges. Hoping to go as a full Indian team along with Danny for the next boomerang world championship in 2026.

PRASANNA MISHRIKOTI, BOOMERANG MAKER & EXPERT - KARNATKA PARTICIPATED IN WORLD CHAMPIONSHIP, KIEL - GERMANY 2016

I met Danny through social media because we share the same passion. He is a multi-talented person and he designs very good and creative rangs and he is popularizing this sport among the young generation with his creative ideas and events which is a great thing in India! boomerang in India has to go a long way, when I was a part of WBC in 2016, there wasn't much awareness about boomerangs in India but today it is different. Personally speaking, Danny is doing a great contribution to boomerang sports in India with his innovative design and the events he conducts for kids and young generations! Love to throw a boomerang with you shortly, all the best Danny

SHISHIR RICHARD JOHN, JHARKHAND D. B

I was on a visit to a neighboring country, Nepal. While on my way to it, I took a short break at Sonauli, India-Nepal border and that's when I first saw some teenagers throwing something which would move away from them only to return within the next some seconds. I was so surprised and excited to see that and therefore wanted to try them myself. I asked Danny and he gave me some tutorials on the same. I brought back home a couple of boomerangs from him and have been practicing and also making my friends and students throw too. Awesome and fun sport.

ABHISHEK JOSHUA, D. B COACH & THROWER - UTTAR PRADESH

I was always a sports person and when I came to know about this amazingly lovely sport called BOOMERANG through Daniel, my first thought was to immediately try my hands on it. Today not only I'm practicing as a self-training exercise, but I'm also training the new throwers. Seeing the current pace of the awareness programs conducted by Daniel's Boomerang, I think India will have at least 20 properly trained teams ready by the end of 2025. Looking forward to continuing my journey with Daniel's Boomerang.

DINESH KUMAR, OWNER - CHAKRA BOOMERANGS, TAMIL NADU

Hello everyone, Boomerang is a very unique sport, and therefore anyone who tries his/her hands on it falls in absolute love with it. Daniel is one of them, he's spreading boomerang very well, congratulations to Dany.

JAMES HOY, BOOMERANG MAKER AND CHAMPION- U. K

I think its a great tool for fitness & for helping focus. It is a natural form of meditation and helps us physically and mentally. Time is irrelevant when throwing, you can lose 6 hours in the blink of an eye, also you meet up with people from all classes, creeds which for me is rather spiritual in nature as it unifies us all. If the whole world threw boomerangs, there would be peace on Earth. One day it will be an Olympic event

KENDALL DAVIS, BOOMERANG MAKER - U. S. A

I strongly relate to what we read in the book of Galatians 6:7-10 from Bible, to boomerangs.

If you live a life of giving and loving, you will receive much in return - just like when a boomerang is thrown properly - and under the right conditions, it returns to you and usually is easy to catch. Conversely, if you live a life of greed and evil intent, you can expect to reap rewards that are not so positive.

If you go out to throw a boomerang, and the first few throws are not well done, you may become discouraged and walk off the field. But, if you continue to practice, and have a good instructor, you will soon be throwing and catching with much better skill, and be a good competitor.

I appreciate Danny's desire to share this new sport with the youth of his community. I see his enthusiasm and joy and how it is infectious to the audience. Good luck to the team.

MANUEL SCHÜTZ, PHYSICIST
MULTIPLE TIMES WORLD BOOMERANG CHAMPION, SWITZERLAND

Boomerangs are a bit of everything: Competition, toy, but also craftsmanship since boomerang throwers usually shape their boomerangs by themself. Some of them focus on performing boomerangs (flying as fast as possible, as long as possible, greatest distance, etc). Many throwers including myself also make boomerangs from naturally bent branches, just for fun.

For a new thrower to competitions, try everything! Make your boomerangs, copy ideas from other throwers, but also make your design. Example: Depending on your throwing technique, find out what's the best wing tip shape for you. Also, go to competitions as early as possible. Regardless of some very low scores, it will be a great experience since the social aspect is as important as winning.

DR. ANITA BENJAMIN, GLOBAL PEACE AMBASSADOR

Mr Daniel Joshua is a Cultural President at National Level of Rashtriya Isai Mahasangh, Pan India Organisation. Also, he is our Cultural and Sports Wings National Official. It would be a proud moment to say he is not only a talented musician but a Composer and lyricist also of modern days. He has excelled in the field of boomerang as a specialist. Our PAN India organization is proud to have him on board. One more thing I would like to mention with pride is that he has written our oath and composed the theme song for RIMNETWORK.

I see a very bright future for the Boomerang sport under Joshua's guidance in bringing it from rural areas to metro cities of the country.

I will try my best to personally connect him with Government and the concerned ministries to help him with his future endeavors come true.

SHIWALI PETER, PRESIDENT -LIONS CLUB ALLD ANGELS

I am in the field of network marketing and a successful leader at Modicare, India. I got invited as a 'Chief Guest' at a boomerang tournament organized by Daniel Joshua. I feel so privileged to have been a part of it. It was heartwarming to see many players from the whole district taking part in the tournament. What surprised me was to see several girl throwers not only taking part in the event but also winning various positions in different categories and therefore grabbing medals and trophies. Boomerang has a nature to return to the thrower after being thrown, similarly Daniel, I would like to say to you that if you are working hard with a true heart, then surely one day all these things will return to you. It will come back and you will be in a good place as you are helping in making the future of many students bright. May God bless you a lot and may you go ahead with your students these are my best wishes.

JOHNSON JOSHUA, BOOMERANG COACH & THROWER - D. B

What makes boomerang sport particularly interesting for me is that it's something that's always evolving. There are new techniques and styles that I can explore and experiment with, so it never feels stale. And it's a great way to connect with nature and appreciate the natural surroundings. Plus, it's a great way to get some exercise and have some fun with friends.

AYXAN ORUJALIYEV, BOOMERANG THROWER - AZERBAIJAN

I like what Danny Joshua a. k. a Daniel Joshua and his team are doing. These people are the pride of India. The people on the Indian team are very pure-hearted. Thank you all for the conversation we keep having and the things you taught me. I hope that one day the Indian team will rise a lot.

GAURAV HUMAN, GRAND MASTER - MARTIAL ARTS & BOOMERANG THROWER, REPRESENTATIVE OF INDIA FOR GERMANY'S ICSSPE & IRAN'S ISDF - LUCKNOW, INDIA

Hello Buddies! Well a short introduction about me. I am a martial artist since the age of 6 and have explored nearly 9 different kinds of martial arts till now and currently on the journey to explore more ahead.
There is a very famous Bollywood movie dialogue by very famous and one of the most successful actors Mr. Shahrukh Khan - " Agar puri shiddat se kisi cheez ko chaho toh poori Kayenaat usey tumse milwane mein lag jati hai" and it turned out to be true once again in my life that childhood fantasy of throwing boomerangs like in the world-famous and every child's favorite character's story of Jungle Book, it's hero Mowgli.

That Mowgli ka 'Panja' which he used to call his boomerang was an amazing weapon he used for protection of himself and the beings of his Jungle Kingdom. The way it used to return to him seemed like magic to every child I am sure and thus it was one of my childhood favorite things I always wanted to own, but unfortunately, it wasn't available anywhere, which made me think that something like this never existed in reality, till one day I saw a program on the discovery channel and realized that they are real and also can be of huge sizes and various designs. I again tried to look for them in Indian Market but they weren't available. This I am talking of the later 90s and even the early years of 2000 (my childhood to teenage time).

Gradually with time as I grew up this boomerang thing got rested back in my thoughts, that maybe one day I will get my hands on it and suddenly one more miracle happened. I saw my dear brother - Daniel, throwing boomerangs in his Facebook posts and I was like wow! That moment was powerful enough to take me back to those childhood and teenage fantasy days when I always wanted to own one and play with it. Soon after Universe started playing its magic and Daniel was in Lucknow city and willing to meet me to expand this boomerang thing across India. Because its awareness as a sport is very limited and so is the availability of the boomerang itself which I very well agree and understand as it took more than 2 decades that I could get an opportunity to hold one in my hand. Daniel and I went to places in Lucknow to try hands-on with it and also do a demonstration of the same in schools & colleges in Lucknow for its awareness.

We have now started meeting small and big groups of people from all age groups and majorly school students and started educating them about this amazing and nearly magical sport of boomerang. Soon we will have lots of Mowglis in India I am sure. I am so happy that this childhood fantasy of mine has finally turned true for being a "Panja" owner/player like Mowgli. Happy Boomeranging! ✨

MICHAEL SIEMS, BOOMERANG MAKER & EXPERT, GERMANY

So we asked Mr. Michael about his views, and he shared in detail about his thoughts on Boomerang 'Under Different Aspects', a must-read.

Cultural - The boomerang plays an important role in Aboriginal culture and it still plays a role in Australia today, although in a very different way.

Mystical - Can you imagine back in the stone age when a human is throwing a piece of wood and it comes back to him? Isn't that mystical? And still is. TRY

Meditative - Go out on a nice field and throw for a while. Not competitive, no practicing for something, just because it is beautiful. Just throw and catch. it's very meditative.

Physical - A returning boomerang is a flying object which uses lift supplied by a certain airfoil when Thrown. Rotation and forward speed distribute this lift at the right position and the right time, so that if everything works together, makes the boomerang return. Magic physics. Try

Historical- The boomerang, an Australian icon, has been found all over the world. Historically, it has a rich heritage spanning various cultures and is renowned for its unique return flight. Study about it.

Archeological - Although the boomerang seems Australian, the oldest boomerang, a non-returner and hunting stick was found around 20000 years ago in Poland, made out of a mammoth tusk. Many more were found all over the world. Try to find one

Philosophical - The boomerang stays for an important saying:
Whatever you throw/say/do comes back to you. Try

Athletic - Throwing a boomerang can be very relaxing, but after a while you feel that it is quite strenuous. But throwing competition is tough. Watch youtube videos e.g. Long Distance thrown by Manuel Schütz or when he threw the world record in Fast Catch. Then you can see how athletic it is. Try

Manufacturing - It is not only mystical, sportive, and just wonderful to throw and catch, you can even make your boomerang and it can be quite easy. There is almost no limit in design and material. It's like a new universe of possibilities. Try

Artistic - You can create artistic boomerangs in many ways.
It can have an artistic painting
artistic shape
artistic design
artistic composition of wood
The making can be artistic itself. Try

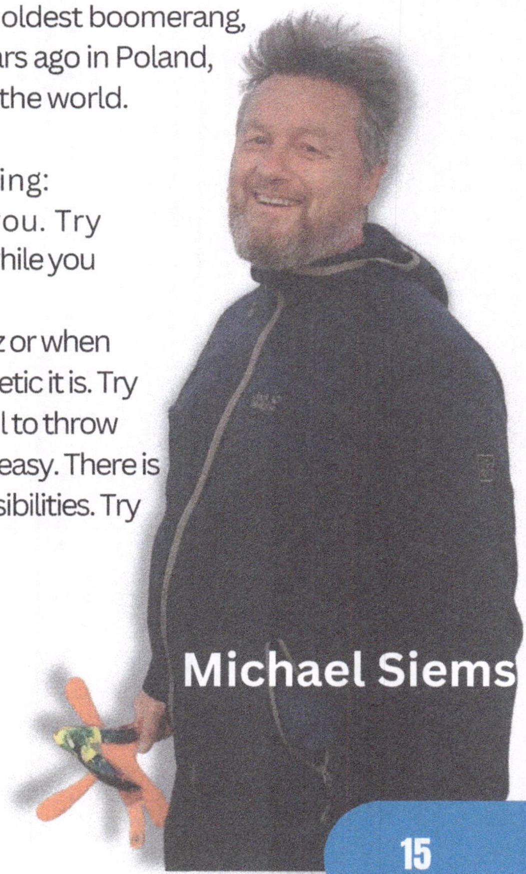
Michael Siems

HEINZ-WILLI DAMMERS, BOOMERANG MAKER & EXPERT, GERMANY

ADMIN - THE WORLD OF BOOMERANG GROUP

At the beginning, boomerang friends from all over the world were able to get to know each other there, meet up and communicate with each other without any major detours. In the past, this was only possible with letters and phone calls. The number of members increased rapidly and more and more people became interested in the boomerang and also became enthusiasts. It was now easy to get all kinds of information and help on the subject. And all newcomers were always warmly welcomed and treated with respect. Countries such as Indonesia and India, where boomerang throwing was not yet so well known, benefited in particular. Now interest was spreading rapidly there too, clubs were founded and large boomerang events are now being organised.

Some people joined our 'small' boomerang family, who are now doing a lot for the boomerang sport in their own countries and are very important for it.
Like the author of this book, Danny Josh*, for example.

He does an incredible amount for the boomerang scene, is very active and has lots of great ideas.

That's why he was voted Member of the Year by the other members in 2023!

I am very proud that my Facebook group has been able to achieve so much and I hope that this will continue!

Boomerangs are totally awesome and super cool! But let's be real, if they're not made right, they just won't fly as well. And when you've got a pro throwing it, man... it's like magic. They make it look so effortless and beautiful. All I can say is, boomerangs are pretty amazing - dynamic and spectacular, that's what they are.

RITESH PITTS - BOOMERANG THROWER, PRAYAGRAJ

*a.k.a Daniel Joshua

Catherine Matheson, Boomerang Enthusiast, Australia

I am honored and grateful to be invited to speak about Boomerang throwing as a Sport.

I am Catherine Matheson, granddaughter of Frank Donnellan (Poppy), who wrote the first rule book for Competitive Boomerang throwing in Australia. He had two wishes, one, everyone on Earth united as one, boomerang throwing, secondly, throwing at an Olympic level, all-inclusive, all abilities, indoor, or outdoor, opening /closing ceremonies. For this, we need men in 75 countries, on 4 continents. For the women, we need 3 continents and 40 countries. We need more women and more countries from both. So far we have the continents.
Thus my interest in the 2032 Brisbane Olympics. You never know we just may achieve this wish with what all Danny and all the other trainers are accomplishing brilliantly these days. Many thanks.
I have recently become more involved with Boomerang Throwing via the BAA, and WABA. I am now 59 +, the usual bone issues and wear and tear of the rest of this old chassis. Minimal exercise. I hadn't thrown booms since the 80s, and that was only a few throws, one perfect return I wasn't game to catch. My boom was one of Poppy's old booms. As a child, I threw often with Poppy. I had the pleasure of throwing at the recent Australian Nationals, the first time I had held a modern boom. So much fun, good people, food, friendships, outside fresh air, exercise. We were all very sore. As an old, female, I did quite well, I was proud. If I can do it, everyone can do it. I am a quiet person, anxious at times, I was welcomed immediately, it was a huge relief, there is no judgment, no assuming, there is patience, kindness, and understanding.
We are all a unique bunch of people, as every boomerang is different, needing different conditions to succeed on its return, we all need care and a tune too. I encourage girls, women, and elders to learn boomerang throwing. The learning environment is a safe environment for anxiety, depression, fear, PTSD, and physical ailments also. Our men boomerang trainers and throwers are honorable, you will be well looked after. Anyone in the boomerang community, throwers, creators, and volunteers are all good people.
Boomerang throwing as a sport or fun activity can be a healing tool, talking, exercise, wheelchair abilities, all abilities, a women's or men's circle to ask for help or recognize someone else needs help. It can be competitive against oneself, or others, it can be creating amazing pieces of artwork, or starting up a wheelchair comp. The actual boomerang is like a peace tool within itself, all the happiness, it always brings back, uniting us all wherever we are.
Encouraging anyone to play or compete in boomerang throwing is such a gift to any recipient, a member of the boomerang throwing community is in a place of safety, fun, a place of healing, mental or physical, a gentle community, caring and kind.

May I give Danny a massive congratulations for all he and his team are accomplishing? Go girls, very good girls I have seen from some of the footage. Well done and thank you for all you are doing in promoting the happy sport of boomerang throwing.

PLAYERS/THROWERS

Sonauli Spartans

Bethel Warriors,
Sonauli

Arya Squad,
Basti

All star,
Anandnagar

Falcon unit,
Basti

Mega Thunder,
Sonauli

The Avengers,
Sonauli

Believers, Prayagraj

Allahabadee Gang, Prayagraj

Team Kanghusri, Kanghushri

Power - Puff Girls, Sonauli

Boom-Hawk, Pharenda

RML Smashers

RML Boomerang Aademy

Team Udaan

Superboys

Team challenger, Betul

Sahara Academy, Lucknow

CURRENT WORK

At 'Daniel's Boomerang,' our unwavering commitment lies in raising awareness about the captivating sport of boomerang. We seize every opportunity to visit diverse communities, including villages, cities, slums, orphanages, educational institutions, government organizations, NGOs, medical professionals, lawyers, officers, politicians, media personnel, children, adolescents, young adults, and the elderly. During these encounters, we patiently impart knowledge about the wonders of boomerangs.

We showcase the mesmerizing flight and return of the boomerang, offering insights into its mechanics and functionality. For those who express interest, we provide engaging workshops and even gift boomerangs to aid in their learning process. Furthermore, we honor dignitaries by presenting them with boomerangs as cherished keepsakes.

Periodically, we organize a spectrum of events, ranging from thrilling boomerang tournaments to immersive workshops where participants can craft their own boomerangs. Exhibitions and awareness sessions are also held to spread knowledge and appreciation for this remarkable sport.

In order to facilitate the exploration of new techniques, we meticulously design and create boomerangs specifically for novice throwers. The gift of our handmade boomerangs never fails to astonish and inspire.

Above all, there is a resounding message that we impart to all - #THROW IT TO KNOW IT. This simple phrase encapsulates the essence of the boomerang experience and encourages individuals to embrace the joy of discovery.

Giving the village kids general information about boomerangs. Also gifted them some.

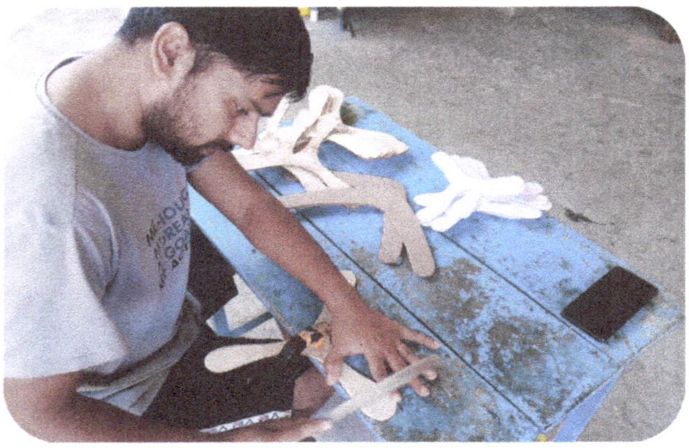

Different shapes of boomerangs being made using only hand tools.

Boomerang workshop at G. S National Academy.

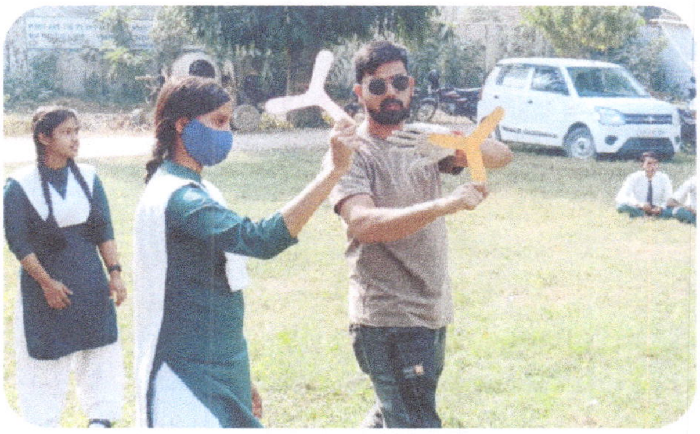

Boomerang workshop at Agricultural Institute of Allahabad.

Boomerang fun time at Bethel Children school.

Boomerang Workshop at Holy Cross school.

Our junior girl thrower teaching the senior girl throwers at a school.

Ready with the team for another workshop at a school.

Telling the youth about boomerangs at a public tea spot. We just met them.

Teaching the local kids as to how a boomerang functions.

Boomerang workshop at a local village with the Village Headman

Teaching boomerang in a public park. These young boys now have their own team.

With the team and the school staff after the boomerang workshop.

Addressing the crowd during a boomerang tournament. Words of encouragement.

A photograph from the training session at M. L. M English School, Jhansi

Talking about the SKY BLADER boomerang by LMI & Fox company from France

School demo about how a boomerang works

Excited students during the workshop at Christ the king college

Workshop at the Blue Bells School, Jhansi

Training time

Photographed during a boomerang tournament.

Trophies for the 6 different categories including Mementos

Junior throwers taking the lead.

One of the throwers making a 'behind the back' catch during the 'Trick Catch' category

Drone shot during a tournament.

Students from Major Dhyanchand Academy Betul, Madhya Pradesh

Gifting a boomerang handmade by me to Shri. M. P Singh ji, Protocol Officer, High Court

Gifting two of my handmade boomerangs to Shri. Prakash D, I. P. S officer

We did a boomerang training workshop with Shri. Aniruddh Singh, Commando trainer and his fitness team.

After a discussion with the officers of the Irrigation department.

Gifted Sister Josephie, principal of Holy Cross School, two of my handmade boomerangs.

Gifted two boomerangs to the Cricket legend Mr. Ashish Nehra (CricRang & Namaste)

Gifted some foreign made boomerangs along with to Sir. Sanjay Ferrow, Principal M. L. M English School

Gifted a traditional and some sports category boomerangs to Fr. Franky, Principal C. K. C

Shri. Rajesh Jaiswal, Chairman - Anandnagar, receiving a traditional shaped boomerang made by me.

Presenting two handmade boomerangs to the State President, B. J. P Madhya Pradesh

Presenting Shri. Vaibhav Singh,
Joint Commissioner - Customs
with the memento for being the chief guest at our boomerang event.

Gifted a traditional handmade boomerang to Sir. Nitin Williams, Principal Blue Bells School

Recieved these Indian themed cardboard boomerangs made and gifted by these star junior throwers.

We made this customized boomerang in honor of all the female throwers around the world.

Joined live on the Grizzly Radio Show, Australia
With other boomerang throwers and coaches from India.

Talking to the girls about boomerangs at
The Hindu Mahila Inter College, Prayagraj

Boomerang training at the Saraswati Vidya Mandir, Prayagraj.

Participated in the Boompop Virtual Boomerang league an international virtual boomerang competition.

Boomerang training session at the J. H College, Betul, Madhya Pradesh

Under 18 boys boomerang summer camp,

Madhya Pradesh

Joined live on the Grizzly Radio Show, Australia
With other boomerang legends from around the world.

Boomerang training session by Sunil Uikey
with the tribal girls.

Junior training session.

Was invited as the Chief Guest on the occasion of
the Sports day finale at St. Joseph's High School.

MEDIA COVERAGE

आधुनिक बूमरैंग के पूर्वज माने जाने वाले ऑस्कर कर्टस एवं हर्ब स्मिथ के सम्मान में डेनियल्स बूमरैंग द्वारा आयोजित हुई जिलास्तरिय बूमरैंग प्रतियोगिता

पूर्वांचल राज्य संवाददाता

महराजगंज। आनंदनगर के एक खेल स्टेडियम मे आयोजित बूमरैंग क्रीड़ा प्रतियोगिता में भाग लेने वालों की संख्या देखकर सभी दर्शक तथा अतिथि गण चकित रह गए। पिछले काफी महीनों से लगातार बूमरैंग खेल के प्रति जागरूकता अभियान चला रहे डेनियल जोशुआ के अपनी उपस्थिति दर्ज करायी तथा खिलाडियों का मनोबल भी बढ़ाया, बताते चलें कि इस रोचक खेल की खास बात यह है कि यह फेंकने वाले के पास पलट कर वापस आ जाता है, मानो इसे फेंका नहीं बल्कि बुलाया गया हो। इसके कार्यप्रणाली को देखकर दर्शकों संग, मुख्य एवं विशिष्ट अतिथि भी किया। खेल समारोह के सफल समापन पर कार्यक्रम के आयोजक डेनियल जोशुआ ने आए हुए मुख्य अतिथि, श्री राजेश जैसवाल, चेयरमैन आनंद नगर और झाँसी एवं रायपुर से विशिष्ट अतिथि के रूप में आयीं श्रीमती संगीता फैरो और डॉ. शानू मसीह को सम्मानित कर उनका हार्दिक धन्यवाद किया।

PURVANCHAL RAJYA 09 DECEMBER 2022

बूमरैंग प्रतियोगिता में कुल 40 खिलाडियों ने किया

हिंद मोर्चा संवाददाता

महराजगंज/फरेन्दा। 06 दिसंबर को मल्टिपरपज़ हॉल, गणेशपुर, जयपुरिया इंटर कॉलेज के बगल में प्रातः 10 बजे बूमरैंग प्रतियोगिता का आयोजन किया गया, प्रतियोगिता के ऑर्गनाइज़र - डैनियल (मेकर, कोच एवं खिलाड़ी, डैनियल्स बूमरैंग के मालिक) रहे। वही आयोजन में मुख्य अतिथि - राजेश जायसवाल, चेयरमैन, नगर पंचायत आनंद नगर तथा विशिष्ट अतिथि-संगीता फैरो, प्रधानाचार्या, झाँसी, शानू मसीह, फिल्म एवं संगीत निर्माता, छत्तीसगढ़, सुनील उईके, अंतरराष्ट्रीय बूमरैंग खिलाड़ी, मध्यप्रदेश जय सिंह यादव, अंतरराष्ट्रीय बूमरैंग खिलाड़ी, उत्तर प्रदेश शामिल रहे।

कुल 40 खिलाडियों ने प्रतिभाग किया

कुल 6 श्रेणियों में प्रथम, द्वितीय एवं तृतीय स्थान के लिए कुल प्रतिभाग किया गया और 18 प्रतिभागियों ने अपनी दावेदारी प्रस्तुत की। जिसने 18 ट्रॉफी, 18 मेडल, 18 सर्टिफिकेट अन्य सभी को प्रतिभाग सर्टिफिकेट वितरित किया गया।

बूमरैंग खेल के बारे मे

महत्वपूर्ण जानकारी

बूमरैंग जब खिलाड़ी हवा में फेंकता है तो वो एक सीमित दूरी तय करके पलट कर फेंकने वाले व्यक्ती के हाथ में आ जाता है। अलग अलग श्रेणी में अलग अलग दूरी, देरी तथा आकार होता है। यह खेल विदेशों मे 50 साल से अधिक समय से खेला जा रहा है। जर्मन स्थित इंटरनेशनल फेडरेशन ऑफ बूमरैंग एसोसिएशन के तहत 40 से अधिक देश हर दो साल पर आयोजित होने वाले वर्ल्डकप में भाग लेते रहते हैं। इस वर्ष अगस्त माह में पहली बार भारत ने भी भाग लिया, जिसमें भारत की ओर से जाने वाले 3 खिलाड़ियों में से 2 खिलाड़ी भी इस जिला स्तरिय प्रतियोगिता में बतौर स्कोरर शामिल हुए। इस प्रतियोगिता के लिए लंदन से स्टार बूमरैंग खिलाड़ी जेम्स होग, स्पेन से अलेओ पलासियो, फ्रांस से एरिक सांग अन्य कई खिलाडियों ने प्रतिभागियों को ढेरों शुभकामनाएं दीं तथा आयोजक

डेनियल ... कहने के ... डेनियल्स ... प्रैक्टाइज़ी ... कार्यक्रम ... रहे। खिला... हबीबा, मो... प्रथम, द्वि... किया। ... मोनिका ... तृतीय स्था... नायक, ... द्वितीय एवं ... में प्रथम ... द्वितीय पर ... बीच वाई... स्थान पर ... के आयो... बातचीत ... क्षेत्र में आ... मेहनत के ... लेना सब...

HINDMORCHA.IN 09 DECEMBER 2022

District level boomerang competition ...

dailyhunt

District level boomerang competition was successfully completed under the banner of Daniel's Boomerang.

Boomerang sports competition was organized in Maharajganj district of Uttar Pradesh on Tuesday, 6th December, in which more than 40 players participated. The players performed very well and brought laurels to the district in different categories.

This competition was organized in honor of Herb Smith and Oscar Cuartas, who are considered to be the forefathers of the modern boomerang game.

Senior players Sunil Uikey and Jai Singh Yadav, who represented India in the Boomerang World Cup held in France this year, played the role of the main scorers of the game.

In the accuracy category, Umme Habiba, Monika Rao and Rajkumar secured the first, second and third positions.
Aamir, Monika and Nandini got 1st, 2nd and 3rd position in fast catch category,
Anurag Nayak, Habiba and Aamir stood first, second and third in the trick catch category,
In the Aussie category, Aditya Dharikar secured the first position, Monika and Aditya Yadav tied for the second position and Arun Yadav secured the third position.

During the competition, Günter Möller, President of the International Federation of Boomerang Associations from Germany, Roger Perry, Vice President from Australia, along with boomerang players from various other countries joined through live broadcast to boost the morale of the players and also congratulated them.

Municipality Chairman Rajesh Jaiswal attended the event as the chief guest and conveyed his good wishes to the Indian throwers. He also tried his hands on the sport.
Educationist Sangeeta Ferrow from Jhansi and filmmaker Shanu Masih from Chhattisgarh also played a special role as the guests of honor and awarded trophies, medals and certificates to the winners and runners-up players.

RajanSafri, the main sponsor of the event, a MasterChef, congratulated all the participants and encouraged them to give their best.
Daniel Joshua, the organizer of the event and the owner of Daniel's Boomerang, expressed his heartfelt gratitude to the guests who were a part of the program and also informed about other district and state level competitions in the coming times.

DAILY HUNT 08 DECEMBER 2022

सोनौली वापसी पर बूमरैंग खिलाड़ी का चेयरमैन सहित सभासदों ने किया सम्मान

पूर्वांचल राज्य ब्यूरो
ब्यूरो चीफ फणीन्द्र कुमार मिश्र की रिपोर्ट

महाराजगंज, सोनौली। बीते सप्ताह तमिलनाडु के चेन्नई शहर मे आयोजित बूमरैंग खेल प्रतियोगिता मे देशभर के विभिन्न राज्यों के बूमरैंग खिलाडियों में हिस्सा लेकर अपना प्रदर्शन किया था जिसकी खबर को पूर्वांचल राज्य (राष्ट्रीय हिंदी दैनिक समाचार पत्र) ने प्रमुखता से अपने अखबार में स्थान दिया था। इसी प्रतियोगिता में उत्तर प्रदेश के महराजगंज जिला के सोनौली नगर निवासी डैनियल जोशुआ ने अपना बेहतरीन प्रदर्शन देते हुए ऑजी. राउन्ड में प्रथम स्थान प्राप्त कर

चेयरमैन हबीब खान ने बेथल चिल्ड्रेन स्कूल के प्रांगण में पहुंच कर माल्यार्पण कर तथा अंगवस्त्र ओढ़ा कर डैनियल को अपनी उपलब्धियों के लिए सम्मानित करने के साथ ही आगामी तमाम अपने हस्त निर्मित बूमरैंग भेंट स्वरूप देते हुए हौसला बढ़ाने के लिए दिली आभार व्यक्त करने साथ ही अपने सीनियर खिलाड़ियों फिलिप सत्यराज (तमिलनाडु) तथा सुनील ऊइके (मध्य प्रदेश) कुमार, शकील, शाहनवाज, अभिषेक, जॉनसन व लोढ़ीया संग बेथल चिल्ड्रेन स्कूल के संस्थापक फादर जोशुआ भी मौजूद रहे।

प्रदूषित पानी दे रहा बीमारी को दावत

पूर्वांचल राज्य ब्यूरो, महाराजगंज, घुघली। महाराजगंज जिला मुख्यालय अंर्तगत ग्राम सभा सिसवा अमहवा मे पेयजल को लेकर ग्रामीणों के समक्ष एक बड़ी समस्या खड़ी हो गई है। इस बाबत कुछ लोगों ने बताया है कि यह इंडिया मार्का हैंडपंप विगत कई वर्षों से बंद पड़ा हुआ है।उन लोगों ने यह भी बताया

PURVANCHAL RAJYA 15/10/23

बूमरैंग खेल किसी जादू से कम नहीं।

09 Dec 2022, 11:11 PM

किसी वस्तु को अपने से दूर फेंके जाने पर वह दूर जाता है ना कि पलटकर वापस आता है, लेकिन महराजगंज जिले के आनंदनगर शहर के मल्टिपरपज़ हॉल स्टेडियम मे हाल ही मे आयोजित एक क्रीड़ा प्रतियोगिता की बात करें तो यह कहना अतिशयोक्ति नहीं होगी कि फेंकी हुई वस्तु काफ़ी दूर जाकर भी वापस आ सकती है वो भी सीधे फेंकने वाले के हाथ मे। है ना रोचक बात?

इस प्रतियोगिता मे 40 से अधिक खिलाडियों ने हिस्सा लिया और काफी अच्छा प्रदर्शन किया। आलम तो यह था कि देखने वाले दर्शकों ने इस हैरतअंगेज खेल को अपने अपने सोशल मीडिया पर लाइव प्रसारित भी कर दिया जिस से अन्य लोग भी देख सकें। .

खेल के दौरान अंतरराष्ट्रीय बूमरैंग फेडरेशन द्वारा फ्रांस मे आयोजित बूमरैंग वर्ल्डकप मे भारत की ओर से खेलने गए खिलाडियों मे से सुनील ऊईके तथा जय सिंह यादव भी बतौर स्कोरर मौजूद रहे। .

09 DECEMBER 2022

दैनिक भारत

डेनियल्स बूमरैंग के तत्वाधान में ज़िला स्तरीय बूमरैंग प्रतियोगिता सफलतापूर्वक हुई संपन्न

By Pragya Singh 09/12/2022 67

बीते मंगलवार दिनाँक 6 दिसंबर को उत्तर प्रदेश के महराजगंज ज़िले मे बूमरैंग खेल प्रतियोगिता का आयोजन किया गया जिसमें कुल 40 से अधिक खिलाड़ियों ने प्रतिभाग किया। खिलाड़ियों ने काफी अच्छा प्रदर्शन करते हुए अलग अलग श्रेणीयों में ज़िले का नाम रौशन किया।।

यह प्रतियोगिता आधुनिक बूमरैंग खेल के पूर्वज माने जाने वाले हर्ब स्मिथ एवं ऑस्कर कर्टस के सम्मान में आयोजित की गई। इस वर्ष फ्रांस मे आयोजित बूमरैंग वर्ल्डकप मे भारत की ओर से खेलने गए सीनियर खिलाड़ी सुनील ऊइके तथा जय सिंह यादव ने खेल के मुख्य स्कोरर की भूमिका निभायी।

एक्यूरेसी श्रेणी में उम्मे ... और राजकुमार ने प्रथम ... स्थान प्राप्त किया। फास्ट ... आमिर, मोनिका और न... एवं तृतीय स्थान, ट्रिक ... नायक, हबीबा तथा आ... एवं तृतीय स्थान पर,ऑ... स्थान पर आदित्य धरीक... मोनिका एवं आदित्य य... हुआ तथा अरुण यादव ... अपना कब्जा जमाया।

DAINIK BHARAT 9 DECEMBER 2022

विद्यार्थियों को सिखाया बूमरैंग खेल का तरीका

झाँसी : अन्तर्राष्ट्रीय बूमरैंग खिलाड़ी एवं कोच डेनियल जोशुआ (नेपाल) तथा सुनील उइके (भोपाल) ने महानगर के मारग्रेट लीस्क मेमोरियल स्कूल, क्राइस्ट द किंग कॉलिज आदि में कार्यशाला आयोजित कर विद्यार्थियों को बूमरैंग खेलने का तरीका सिखाया। उन्होंने बताया कि बूमरैंग लकड़ी, पॉलिमर या फाइबर से बना होता है, जिसे हवा में फेंकने पर सीमित दूरी कर वापस खिलाड़ी के हाथ में आ जाता है। इसका विश्वकप भी आयोजित होता है। जंगल बुक मूवी के मुख्य किरदार मोगली ने विश्वभर में प्रसिद्ध किया है। उन्होंने बताया कि इस सप्ताह झाँसी के अन्य विद्यालयों में भी कार्यशाला आयोजित कर ऐसे खिलाड़ियों का चयन किया जाएगा, जो जिला, राज्य एवं राष्ट्रीय

DAINIK JAGRAN 30/04/2024 JHANSI

विदेश से बूमरैंग खेल से नाता रखने वाले नामी गिरामी दिग्गजों ने के खिलाड़ियों ने जिले का रौशन किया ।

LOKBHARTI NEWS 09 DECEMBER 2022

डेनियल जोशुआ ने छात्रों,युवाओं को बूमरैंग खेल की जानकारी देते हुए खेल के प्रति जागरूक किया

महराजगंज:सोमवार को सरदार पटेल इन्टरमीडियेट कॉलेज, लक्ष्मीपुर के ग्राउंड पर सोनौली बेथल चिल्ड्रेन स्कूल के छात्रों एवं बूमरैंग टीम संग डेनियल्स बूमरैंग के मालिक डेनियल जोशुआ ने वहाँ के छात्रों, युवाओं एवं ग्राम प्रधान से मुलाकात कर बूमरैंग खेल से संबंधित जानकारी देते हुए खेल के प्रति जागरूक किया।

जल्द ही एक गोष्ठी का आयोजन कर बड़े स्तर पर बूमर.. प्रतियोगिता करवाने के लिए अपने भरपूर समर्थन का वाद। किया।

डेनियल जोशुआ ने अपने द्वारा हस्त निर्मित बूमरैंग तोहफे के रूप में ग्राम प्रधान को भेंट दिया तथा उनसे खुद हवा मे भी उड़वाया। बूमरैंग खेल का प्रदर्शन सोनौली के बेथल चिल्ड्रेन स्कूल के जोनसन सर, अभिषेक सर, छात्रों मे अनुराग नायक, नंदनी गौड़, हबीबा, आदित्य, यश, आमिर संग अनु ने किया।

04 OCTOBER 2022

LIVE TV SAMACHAR 07 DECEMBER 2022

हिन्द मोर्चा संवाददाता

महराजगंज/नौतनवां। सोनौली नगर पंचायत अध्यक्ष हबीब खान द्वारा भारतीय बूमरैंग खिलाड़ी डैनियल जोशुआ को सम्मानित किया गया. बीते सप्ताह तमिलनाडु के चेन्नई शहर में आयोजित बूमरैंग खेल प्रतियोगिता में देशभर के विभिन्न राज्यों के बूमरैंग खिलाड़ियों नें हिस्सा लेकर अपना प्रदर्शन किया। इसी प्रतियोगिता में उत्तर प्रदेश के महराजगंज ज़िला के सोनौली नगर निवासी डैनियल जोशुआ ने अपना बेहतरीन प्रदर्शन देते हुए ऑजी राउन्ड में प्रथम स्थान प्राप्त कर जिले का नाम रौशन किया। खेल प्रतियोगिता में हिस्सा लेने के बाद नगर में वापसी पर सोनौली नगर पंचायत के मुखिया, चेयरमैन हबीब खान ने बेथल चिल्ड्रेन स्कूल के

डैनियल ने अध्यक्ष को भेंट किया हस्त निर्मित बूमरैंग

डैनियल ने भी नगर अध्यक्ष को अपने हस्त निर्मित बूमरैंग भेंट स्वरूप देते

HINDMORCHA NEWS 16/10/23

TV1 INDIA NEWS 08 DECEMBER 2022

डेनियल्स बूमरैंग द्वारा आयोजित हुयी जिलास्तरीय बूमरैंग प्रतियोगिता

लोक भारती न्यूज़ ब्यूरो

महराजगंज। जनपद महराजगंज के आनंदनगर के खेल स्टेडियम मे आयोजित बूमरैंग क्रीड़ा प्रतियोगिता का आयोजन किया लाइव प्रसारण के जरिए अपनी उपस्थिति दर्ज करायी तथा खिलाडियों का मनोबल भी बढ़ाया, बताते चलें कि इस रोचक खेल की खास बात यह है कि यह फेंकने वाले के पास पलट कर वापस आ

LOKBHARTI NEWS

बृजमनगंज(एसएनबी)। जुलाई माह के आखिरी दिन महात्मा गांधी इंटर कालेज विद्यालय, बृजमनगंज में बूमरैंग खेल की जागरुकता कार्यशाला का आयोजन हुआ। जिन लोगों को नहीं मालूम कि बूमरैंग क्या है उन्हें बता दें कि बूमरैंग एक ऐसा खेल है जो अंतर्राष्ट्रीय स्तर पर 50 वर्षो से भी अधिक समय से खेला जा रहा है और इस खेल का जर्मनी स्थित अंतर्राष्ट्रीय बूमरैंग फेडरेशन द्वारा विश्व कप का आयोजन भी होता है।

इस खेल की खासियत यह है कि सही दिशा और सही तरीके से फेंके जाने पर बूमरैंग एक सीमित दूरी तय कर फेंकने वाले खिलाड़ी के पास पलट कर वापस आ जाता है। जागरुकता अभियान के दौरान बूमरैंग टीम के अध्यापकों तथा युवा विद्यार्थियों को खेल विभिन्न श्रेणियों, उनके नियम तथा विभिन्न आकार के बूमरैंग और उनके निर्माताओं के बारे में भी जानकारी दी। 20 मीटर से लेकर

जागरूकता कार्यशाला

200 मीटर से भी अधिक दूरी तय कर सकता है बूमरैंग। मौखिक जानकारी देने इसके बाद डैनियल ने विद्यालय के प्रबंधक आशीष जायसवाल तथा प्रधानाचार्य डा. राम अवतार को भी बूमरैंग फेंकना सिखाया तथा संग मे आये टीम के कोच अभिषेक ने नये विद्यार्थियों को इस खेल का प्रशिक्षण दिया। लगभग 500 से अधिक युवा विद्यार्थियों ने इस खेल के प्रति अपनी खास रुचि दिखायी जिसमें

RASHTRIYA SAHARA 01/08/23

हिन्द मोर्चा संवाददाता

महराजगंज/ नौतनवां। बेथल चिल्ड्रेन स्कूल एवं महराजगंज जिले तथा उत्तर प्रदेश के लिए बड़े ही गर्व की बात है कि सोनौली बेथल चिल्ड्रेन स्कूल के डेनियल जोशुआ द्वारा निर्मित तथा गाया हुआ गीत «मेरा देश है वीरों वाला» का विमोचन 21 जनवरी को राज्यपाल आनंदीबेन पटेल के द्वारा किया गया. डेनियल के गाने को सुनकर वहां उपस्थित लोगों ने डेनियल जोशुआ की काफी सराहना की. आपको बता दे कि डेनियल जोशुआ एक बूमरैंग खिलाड़ी भी है और वह अपनी प्रतिभा से अपने क्षेत्र तथा जिलें का नाम लगातार विश्व पटल पर लाने का काम करते रहते है.उनके द्वारा रचित देश भक्ति गीत का प्रसारण दुरदर्शन टीवी के माध्यम से राष्ट्रीय स्तर पर 26 जनवरी परेड ग्राउंड से उसका सीधा प्रसारण किया जाएगा. जिसको लगभग 15 करोड़ लोग एक साथ सुन सकेंगे. इस गीत के लिए उन्हें मुंबई में सम्मानित भी किया जाएगा। उनके इस उपलब्धि पर बेथल चिल्ड्रेन स्कूल के अध्यापकों एवं क्षेत्र के लोगों ने उनको ढेरों बधाइयां दी.बेथल चिल्ड्रेन स्कूल के प्रबंधक ने बताया कि हमारा स्कूल हमेशा से ही समाज को सशक्त करने के लिए तत्पर था और रहेगा।

HINDMORCHA 27 JANUARY 2023

TV1 INDIA NEWS 12/05/2023

NEWS 9 BHARAT, 09/03 2023

भारतीय बूमरैंग खिलाड़ी एवँ बूमरैंग निमार्ता ने नए अंदाज में मनाया अंतरराष्ट्रीय महिला दिवस

PURVANCHAL RAJYA 10/03/2023

भारतीय बूमरैंग खिलाड़ी एवँ बूमरैंग निर्माता, डैनियल जो...
ने बिल्कुल नए अंदाज में मनाया अंतरराष्ट्रीय महिला दिवस

HINDMORCHA 10/03/2023

सोनौली के डैनियल जोशुआ ने मध्य प्रदेश के भाजपा प्रदेश अध्यक्ष से बूमरैंग खेल को बढ़ावा देने के लिए की मुलाकात.

हिन्दमोर्चा न्यूज़ महराजगंज सदर.

उत्तर प्रदेश के सोनौली नगर के डैनियल जोशुआ ने मध्य प्रदेश के प्रदेश अध्यक्ष से बूमरैंग खेल को बढ़ावा देने के लिए की मुलाकात, भेंट किए हस्त निर्मित बूमरैंग। बूमरैंग एक अंतरराष्ट्रीय खेल है जो की पिछले 5 दशकों से विश्वभर में खेला जा रहा है। लेकिन भारत में इसकी लगभग ना के बराबर जानकारी है. इसलिए डैनियल्स बूमरैंग की टीम पिछले वर्ष से लगातार विभिन्न जगहों पर समय समय पर कार्यशालाओं तथा जागरूकता अभियानों को आयोजित कर इस खेल के

HIND MORCHA 30/05/2023

TV1 INDIA NEWS 11 MARCH 2023

प्रयागराज। किसी जादू से कम नहीं 'बूमरैंग' जो फेंके जाने पर काफी दूर जाने के बावजूद पलट कर वापस आता है। केवल उत्तर प्रदेश भर में 2000 से अधिक लोगों को प्रशिक्षण दे चुके हैं डैनियल जिसमें से 100 से अधिक लोग इसमे बूमरैंग जगत की कम्यूनिटी ने काफी सराहा। डैनियल का यह सपना है कि आने वाले वर्ष 2024 में हवाई, अमेरिका में होने वाले विश्वकप में भारत की ओर से एक जूनियर और एक सीनियर टीम को लेकर प्रतिभाग करें और यही कारण है कि वो इस खेल देशभर में इस खेल के प्रति जागरूकता अभियान चलाने की कड़ी मे प्रयागराज के विभिन्न जगहों पर डैनियल्स बूमरैंग की टीम द्वारा ट्रेनिंग कैम्प का आयोजन किया गया जिसमें बच्चों, युवाओं तथा महिलाओं ने भी बढ़चढ़कर हिस्सा लिया। बूमरैंग को

SWATANTRA CHETNA - 07 APRIL 2023

दैनिक मत ⏮ दामजीपुरा, जाहिद खान

शासकीय महाविद्यालय भीमपुर में अंतरराष्ट्रीय स्तर के बूमरैंग खिलाड़ी राहुल उईके द्वारा बच्चों को बूमरैंग खेल के विषय में मार्गदर्शन दिया गया था। इस कार्यक्रम का आयोजन आजादी का अमृत महोत्सव समिति एवं

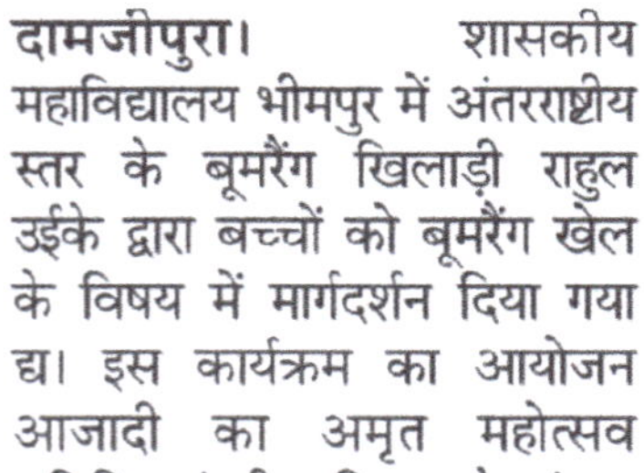

दामजीपुरा। शासकीय महाविद्यालय भीमपुर में अंतरराष्ट्रीय स्तर के बूमरैंग खिलाड़ी राहुल उईके द्वारा बच्चों को बूमरैंग खेल के विषय में मार्गदर्शन दिया गया था। इस कार्यक्रम का आयोजन आजादी का अमृत महोत्सव

देशभर में तेज़ी के साथ बढ़ रही है बूमरैंग खेल के प्रति जागरूकता, महराजगंज से पिछले वर्ष हुई थी शुरुआत

बूमरैंग खेल के जागरुकता कार्यशाला का आयोज...

AMAR BHASKAR 01/08/2023

मध्य प्रदेश पहुंची डेनियल्स टीम

जासं, नौतनवा: सोनौली कस्बा के रहने वाले बूमरैंग खेल के संस्थापक डैनियल जोशुआ रविवार को मध्य प्रदेश के भाजपा प्रदेश अध्यक्ष विष्णुदत्त शर्मा से मिलकर उन्हें हस्तनिर्मित परंपरागत तथा आधुनिक बूमरैंग भेंट की।

संस्थापक डैनियल जोशुआ ने बताया कि बूमरैंग अब अंतरराष्ट्रीय से विश्वभर में खेला जा रहा है। बूमरैंग एक छड़ी है जो खिलाड़ी द्वारा फेंकने पर वापस उसके पास लौट आती है। भारत में इसकी नहीं के बराबर जानकारी है। डैनियल्स बूमरैंग की टीम विभिन्न जगहों पर पहुंचकर कार्यशालाओं का आयोजन कर रही है। बताया कि मध्य प्रदेश के 10 जिलों में समर

DAINIK JAGRAN 29/05/23

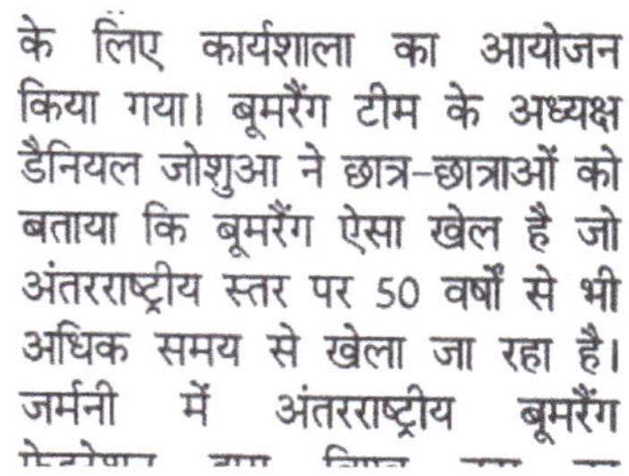

के लिए कार्यशाला का आयोजन किया गया। बूमरैंग टीम के अध्यक्ष डैनियल जोशुआ ने छात्र-छात्राओं को बताया कि बूमरैंग ऐसा खेल है जो अंतरराष्ट्रीय स्तर पर 50 वर्षों से भी अधिक समय से खेला जा रहा है। जर्मनी में अंतरराष्ट्रीय बूमरैंग

DAINIK JAGRAN 01/08/23

Gratitude and appreciation -
The OCBF' s impact on our boomerang journey

As I embarked on my journey with sport boomerang in December 2021, I was struck by the warmth and camaraderie of the global boomerang community. Throwers, boomsmiths, and enthusiasts from around the world generously shared their experiences, expertise, and passion with me, fueling my desire to explore this fascinating sport further.

One organization that has played a particularly significant role in my boomerang journey is the **Oscar Cuartas Boomerang Foundation (OCBF)**. Under the visionary leadership of its President, **Dr. Dara Cuartas**, the OCBF has been tirelessly working to strengthen the global boomerang community. Their efforts have been instrumental in promoting the sport, fostering connections among enthusiasts, and celebrating the artistry and craftsmanship of boomsmiths.

One of the OCBF's most notable initiatives is the **Aesthetic Competition**, held annually at the World Boomerang Championship since 2012. This showcase of extraordinary art, craft, and boomsmith work has become a beloved tradition, highlighting the creativity and skill of boomerang enthusiasts worldwide. The awards feature categories including Craftsmanship, Decoration, Natural Elbow, Throwstick, Boomerang Related Object, and Best of the Show. These categories showcase the diversity and artistry of boomerang design, honoring the skills and imagination of boomsmiths and artisans worldwide.

Koko Handoko won First Prize in the Decoration Category, USA WBC 2024

Peter Hansch won Craftmanship and Best Overall category at Kiel, Germany WBC 2016

Torsten Grunde won Natural Elbow at Colorado USA WBC 2024

Eckward Mawick,won Natural Elbow, Kiel, Germany WBC 2016

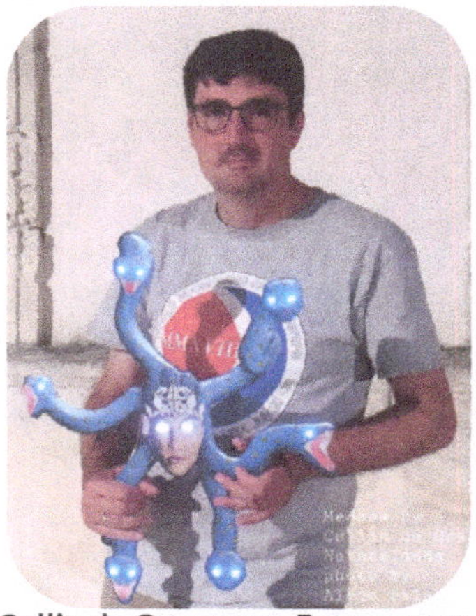

Collin de Graag won Boomerang Decoration and Best Overall at WBC 2022

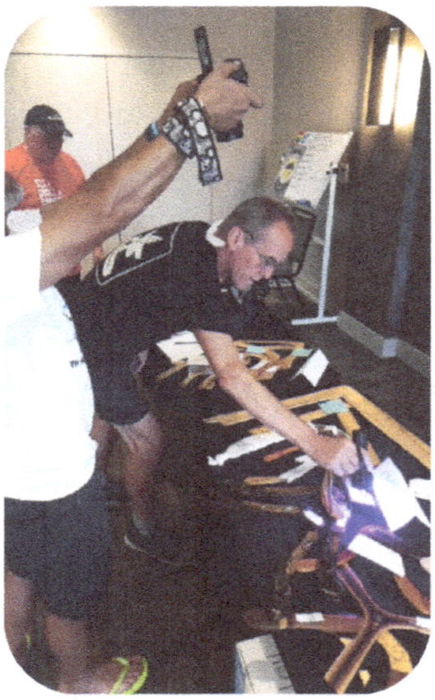

Various photographs during the Aesthetic Events

I am deeply grateful to the OCBF for their unwavering support of our boomerang tournaments, held annually in honor of Boomerang Masters Oscar Cuartas and Herb Smith. The foundation's sponsorship of all three tournaments has been instrumental in their success, allowing us to bring together throwers, boomsmiths, and enthusiasts from around the world to celebrate our shared passion for the sport.

The OCBF's generosity and dedication to the boomerang community are a testament to the transformative power of sport and the importance of nurturing connections among like-minded individuals. I am honored to acknowledge their contributions to our tournaments and to the global boomerang community, and I look forward to continuing our collaboration in the years to come.

Posters, banners & Event photos

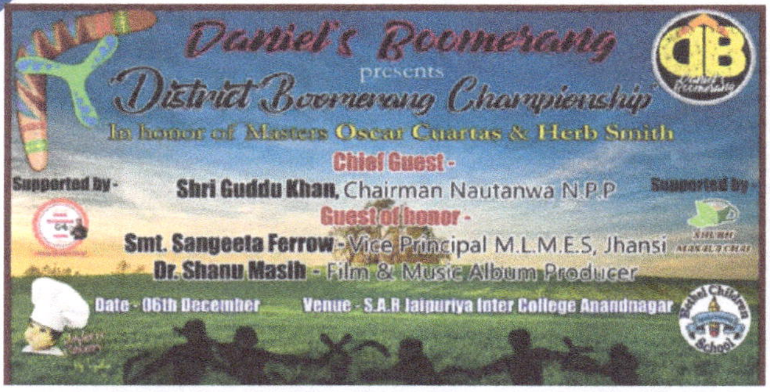

Some of our work, but most of these designs are from the world's top boomerang makers. So here are the photos of some of our...

SELF MADE BOOMERANGS

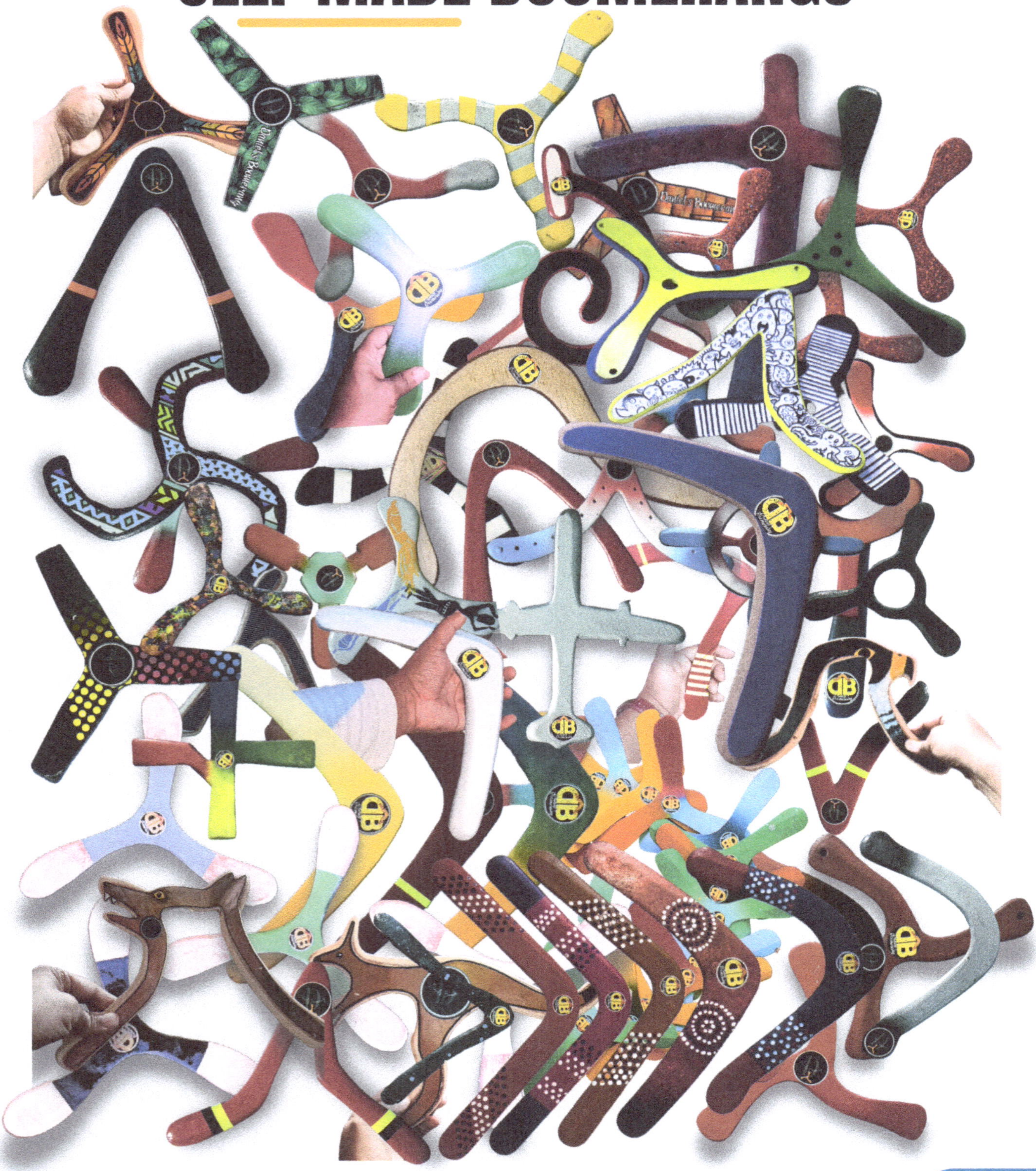

D.I.Y

Note: The below-illustrated guide is for a right-handed boomerang thrower.
For a left-handed boomerang, kindly do the same, just in a mirror image.
For further information, kindly contact us and we will help.

LET'S LEARN HOW TO MAKE A RETURNING BOOMERANG USING CARDBOARD OR THICK PAPER/PLASTIC.

Print this boomerang template using any printer on an A4 sheet

Using glue, paste the printout on a used empty cereal box (cornflakes, chocos, etc)

Using a scissor cut the printed shape out.

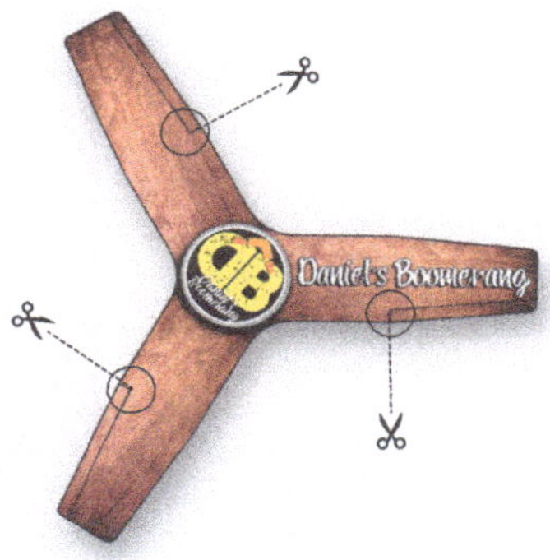

Make a small straight cut at the marked area on all the three wings (approx. 1cm)

Now place the boomerang on a flat surface and bend down the 'blue dotted line' part of the edge, on all three boomerang wings. (nearly 15°)

Hold it vertical and throw it.

Throw it, to know it

Scan this QR code to watch the video tutorial or use the URL
https://t.ly/gxHX

Download the boomerang templates by either scanning this QR code or by using the link address below. Print on an A4 size paper.
https://rb.gy/eluung

PROMOTIONAL & GIFT PRODUCTS

'THROW IT TO KNOW IT' TEES

For throwers

D. B TEES

For D. B team

D. B KEYRINGS & EARRINGS

D. B CAR PERFUME

D. B PLAYING CARDS

CUSTOM TROPHIES & MEMENTOS

DAILY WEAR TEES

INDOOR FUN BOOMERANGS

TRADITIONAL SHAPED BOOMERANGS FOR DIGNITARIES

Our own models/designs

Namaste

This boomerang embodies the spirit of the traditional Indian greeting, featuring carefully designed aerofoils that ensure a smooth return to the thrower. Each piece is meticulously hand-painted, adding a touch of artistry to its functionality

Mowgli

Inspired by the famous Jungle Book story and in honor of the Gond tribe of Madhya Pradesh, this accurately returning boomerang pays homage to the adventure and wilderness of the Indian jungle.

Anteater

This boomerang's unique shape resembles the long snout of an anteater, giving it a distinct and eye-catching appearance. The design was carefully painted to accentuate the snout-like look, making it both visually appealing and aerodynamically efficient

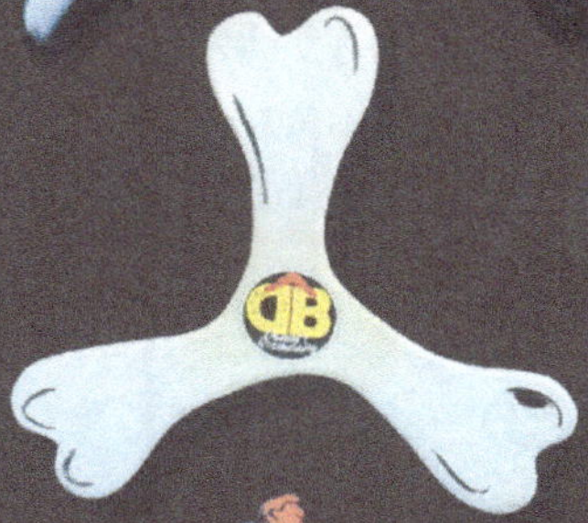

Backbone

As our first ever self-designed model, Backbone's shape resembles a bone. With its ability to return to the thrower, it earned its name with the suggestion of my friend, Victor Poulin from the United States.

CricRang

The perfect catch! The 'Cric Rang' boomerang combines passion for cricket with aerodynamic design. Celebrating the Indian Cricket Team's 2024 World Cup win, this unique boomerang features a bowler, batsman, and wicket keeper in a thrilling moment of play.

Pranam

Similar to the Namaste model, Pranam possesses a slightly lighter build and exhibits a different flight pattern. While still capturing the essence of the traditional Indian greeting, Pranam offers a unique and powerful experience when thrown

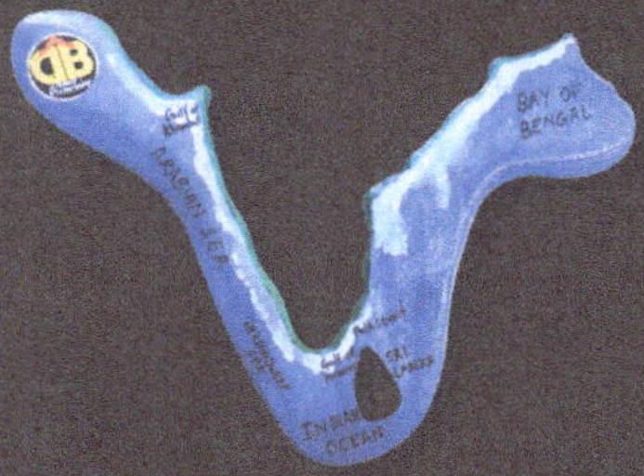

Indian Peninsula

Where geography meets aerodynamics! Say hello to the 'Indian Peninsula' boomerang, a meticulously crafted tribute to India's unique landscape. Shaped like the lower part of the Indian map. And with its perfect return, it's a joy to fly.

and many more

INDIA Runathon
CHAK DE INDIA WALK RUN MARATHON
CERTIFICATE
Daniel Joshua

INDIA RUNATHON
CERTIFICATE
OF ACHIEVEMENT
THIS IS TO CERTIFY THAT
Daniel Joshua
OFFICIAL WORLD RECORD HOLDER

CERTIFICATE
OF APPRECIATION
DANIEL JOSHUA

This is to Certify and Honour
Daniel Joshua

CERTIFICATE
OF EXCELLENCE
Daniel Joshua

WORLD RECORD

I am thrilled to announce that the Daniel's Boomerang team, consisting of myself, Sunil Uikey, Johnson, Abhishek, and Michael Joshua, has accomplished an extraordinary milestone that has set an official world record. In collaboration with thousands of fellow Indians, we participated in a marathon organized by India Runathon for charity. Together, we covered a remarkable distance of 10 kms within a span of 24 hours. This collective effort, characterized by the involvement of numerous individuals from our country, enabled us to establish a new record for the highest number of people from a single nation accomplishing such a remarkable feat. Our unwavering commitment, perseverance, and remarkable teamwork exemplify the essence of this achievement, all while positively impacting the lives of those in need. Through our endeavor, we aspire to inspire readers to pursue their dreams, embrace teamwork, and harness the capacity to make a profound change in the world around them.

INDIA RUNATHON
CERTIFICATE
OF ACHIEVEMENT
THIS IS TO CERTIFY THAT
Michael Joshua
OFFICIAL WORLD RECORD HOLDER

INDIA RUNATHON
CERTIFICATE
OF ACHIEVEMENT
THIS IS TO CERTIFY THAT
Johnson Joshua
OFFICIAL WORLD RECORD HOLDER

INDIA RUNATHON
CERTIFICATE
OF ACHIEVEMENT
THIS IS TO CERTIFY THAT
Sunil Uikey
OFFICIAL WORLD RECORD HOLDER

INDIA RUNATHON
CERTIFICATE
OF ACHIEVEMENT
THIS IS TO CERTIFY THAT
Abhishek Joshua
OFFICIAL WORLD RECORD HOLDER

Appreciation Letters

LIONS CLUB ALLAHABAD ANGELS

Lion Shiwali Anjla Peter, President | Lion Anjana Shukla, Secretary | Lion Usha Gupta, Treasurer

harter President ION PRATIBHA SAHAI
nm. Past President ION MADHVI AGRAWAL
st Vice President ION ARUNA ASTHANA
nd Vice President ION TRAPTI PANWAR
rd Vice President ION PREMLATA PRASAD
oint Secretary ION RIJU LAL
oint Treasurer ION VANDANA TIWARI
ail Twister ION ALPONA SARKAR
amer ION ANITA KESARWANI
R.O ION KAKOLI WILLIAMS
lembership Chairperson ON ALKA JAISWAL
IF Coordinator ON RITA [illegible] DWIVEDI
ub Service Chairperson ON ALPONA ROY
Marketing & Communication Chairperson ON RACHNA MISHRA
Chairperson ON ABHA JAISWAL
ub health Chairperson ON MEERA SINGH
oard of Directors ON MADHAVI AGRAWAL, ON MAMTA BANSAL, ON PRAMILA SINGH, ON ALKA JAISWAL, ON RITA DWIVEDI, ON MITHLESH AGRAWAL, ON SEEMA SINGH, ON MANJUSHREE SINGH, ON SUNANDITA BANARJEE, ON MAYA DWIVEDI, ON ABHA SARAN, ON PRATIMA SINGH, ON PRATIBHA SAHAI, ON MAMTA SINGH, ON ARUNA ASTHANA, ON ALPANA ROY

Ref. AL/DB   Date 12/9/2

Dear Daniel Joshua,

I am writing to express my heartfelt appreciation and pride for your outstanding achievements and contributions to the sport of Boomerang. It is hard to believe that it was just a few years ago when I first introduced you to this fascinating sport. Your passion and dedication have taken you to great heights, and I couldn't be prouder!

Your innovative designs, new ideas, and events have not only promoted the sport but also taken it to a whole new level. Your enthusiasm is contagious, and you have inspired many to take up the sport. I am thrilled to see your progress and the impact you have made.

As the President of Lions Club Allahabad Angels, I am delighted to see our club's values of innovation, community service, and fellowship reflected in your work. Your tireless efforts to popularize Boomerang have brought people together, fostering a sense of community and camaraderie.

Please accept my warmest congratulations and best wishes for your future endeavors. I offer my blessings and support as you continue to soar to new heights. May your passion for Boomerang continue to inspire and uplift others.

Keep shining, Daniel! You are a true champion and a role model for many.

With pride and appreciation,

Lion Shiwali Peter
President, Lions Club Allahabad Angels
Prayagraj

Mrs. Shiwali Peter
President - Lions Club, Allahabad Angels

Date:21-09-2024

TO WHOM IT MAY CONCERN

LETTER OF APPRECIATION

I am delighted to express my heartfelt appreciation to Mr. Daniel Joshua, Founder of Daniel's Boomerang, for his outstanding contributions to promoting the sport of Boomerang in India and globally.

Mr. Joshua's tireless efforts in organizing numerous training workshops and tournaments have provided a platform for young enthusiasts to showcase their skills and talent. His initiatives have not only elevated the sport to new heights but also inspired a new generation of players.

I commend Mr. Joshua for his innovative approach in designing Boomerangs that reflect Indian culture, such as the "Namaste", "Pranam", and "Mogli" designs, which have earned him the distinction of being India's first Boomerang designer.

His dedication to promoting the sport, coupled with his passion for empowering youth, has made a significant impact on the lives of many. I acknowledge his contributions and express my gratitude for his selfless service to the sport.

Please accept my warmest congratulations and best wishes for your future endeavors.

Sincerely,

21.09.24

[Divyakant Singh Rathore]
Additional Chief Judicial Magistrate,
Gautam Buddha Nagar (U.P.)

The honorable Divyakant Singh Rathore

Additiona Chief Judicial Magistrate, Gautam Buddha Nagar

MARGARET LEASK MEMORIAL ENGLISH SCHOOL
(Affiliated to the Council for Indian School Certificate Examinations, New Delhi)
DIOCESE OF LUCKNOW
CHURCH OF NORTH INDIA

MATTHEW 6:33

Date ....

To,
Mr. Daniel Joshua,
Founder,
Daniel Institute of Arts,
Daniel's Boomerang India
& U.P. Boomerang Association

Dear Sir,

I am pleased to invite you to conduct a three days workshop on promoting Boomerang at Margaret Leask Memorial English School. The workshop will be based on training the students about the skills of Boomerang. The dates for the workshop will be 22, 23, 24 April 2024.

I very much look forward to hearing from you and hope that you would be willing to accept our invitation to this very important event.

Mr. Sanjay Ferrow
Principal,
Margaret Leask Memorial English School,
Jhansi. (U.P.)

PRINCIPAL
MARGARET LEASK MEMORIAL ENGLISH SCHOOL
C.P. MISSION COMPOUND

Mr. Sanjay Ferrow
Principal - M.L.M.E School, Jhansi

CROWN MALL
A unit of Goel Builders

FUN | FOOD | MOVIES | SHOPPING

Mr Daniel Joshua
Daniel's Boomerang

Dear Mr Daniel Joshua

We would like to extend our heartfelt appreciation for participating in our recent festive event at Crown Mall. Your demonstration of boomerangs was truly captivating, and we were impressed by the team's enthusiasm and expertise

The insights your team shared about the history and cultural significance of boomerangs, particularly in relation to Southern India, were enlightening for our visitors. The live demonstration of short-range boomerangs was nothing short of magical, and we received overwhelmingly positive feedback from the audience

Your interaction with our visitors added a unique dimension to the event, and we are grateful for the time and effort you invested in making it a memorable experience for everyone involved

We would love to have Team Daniel's Boomerang back at Crown Mall in the future. We believe that having a stall would be a great way to showcase your products and expertise, and we would be more than happy to support you in promoting the art of boomerang-making and throwing

Please let us know if you're interested in collaborating with us further, and we can discuss potential opportunities for future events or promotions

Once again, thank you for sharing your passion and expertise with us. We look forward to the possibility of working with you again

Best regards,

For Goel Builders

Mr Yogendra Arya (Mall G.M)

CROWN MALL

Mr. Yogendra Arya
G. M Crown Mall, Lucknow

सत्यमेव जयते

Dear **Daniel**,

It is my pleasure to mention that your effort to revive the ancient sport of Boomerang, among the youths present in the hinterland of Indo-Nepal border is not only commendable but appreciable too. It takes lots of grit, motivation and dedication to leave the comforts and glitters of cities to move towards the real Bharat and do which is unheard or never been tried. Your effort to design new form of boomerangs resembles your creativity and your zeal to excel in your life.

Your passion to inspire the youths and reminding them about our heritage sport will have a far-reaching impact, which will surely take this sport to a new height.

Godspeed !

Vaibhav Kumar Singh, IRS
Joint Commissioner
CBIC, DoR, MoF
Government Of India

Mr. Vaibhav Kumar Singh
Joint Commissioner - DoR

To
Mr. Daniel Joshua
President, Boomerang Association of India
Alambagh, Lucknow
Uttar Pradesh – 226005

Date: July 25, 2025

Subject: Heartfelt Appreciation for Your Pioneering Work in Reviving Boomerang Sport

Dear Mr. Joshua,

As a selector in cricket, I have witnessed first-hand how sports can transcend boundaries, uplift communities, and ignite passion across generations. I write to express my deepest appreciation for your extraordinary commitment to reviving and promoting the sport of boomerang in India.

Your relentless efforts—particularly in bringing this unique and ancient sport from the heartlands of rural Uttar Pradesh to national attention—are nothing short of remarkable. By reconnecting India with a game rooted in tribal heritage, you are not only preserving cultural legacy but also inspiring a new generation of athletes to embrace something truly original.

The Boomerang Association of India, under your visionary leadership, is setting the stage for a historic sporting resurgence. Much like cricket once found its footing and flourished across the country, I believe boomerang is poised to spark a similar movement—thanks to the groundwork you are laying.

Your passion, perseverance, and grassroots engagement are commendable, and I have no doubt that your journey will leave a lasting impact on India's sporting landscape.

Wishing you continued success as you guide this sport toward national recognition and beyond.

Warm regards,
Ashish Winston Zaidi
Selector, Uttar Pradesh Cricket Association

Mr. Ashish Winston Zaidi
Selector, Uttar Pradesh Cricket ASsociation

प्रिय डैनियल,

आपने जिस समर्पण और साहस के साथ भारत-नेपाल सीमा के दूरदराज़ क्षेत्रों में रहने वाले युवाओं के बीच प्राचीन बूमरैंग खेल को पुनर्जीवित करने का बीड़ा उठाया है, वह अभूतपूर्व, अनुकरणीय और राष्ट्रभक्ति से परिपूर्ण कार्य है।

आज के समय में जब युवा शहरी चमक-धमक और सुविधाओं की ओर आकर्षित होते हैं, आपने उन्हें मूल भारत से जोड़ने, उनकी जड़ों और सांस्कृतिक विरासत की पहचान कराने का जो कार्य किया है, वह अत्यंत सराहनीय है।

आपका यह प्रयास कि आप बूमरैंग के आधुनिक स्वरूप को डिज़ाइन कर रहे हैं, न केवल आपकी रचनात्मक सोच और तकनीकी समझ को दर्शाता है, बल्कि यह भी प्रमाणित करता है कि आप में अपने देश और इसकी परंपराओं के लिए गहरी निष्ठा और प्रेरणा है।

आपका यह अभियान केवल एक खेल को पुनर्जीवित करने का नहीं, बल्कि युवाओं को दिशा, आत्मबल और राष्ट्रीय गौरव से जोड़ने का सशक्त माध्यम बन रहा है। मुझे पूर्ण विश्वास है कि यह कार्य आने वाले समय में नई पीढ़ी के लिए प्रेरणा-स्तंभ बनेगा।

आपको मेरी ओर से हार्दिक शुभकामनाएँ और अभिनंदन,
कि आप इसी तरह राष्ट्र सेवा में समर्पित रहें और भारत का नाम गौरव से ऊँचा करें।

वंदे मातरम्।

ANIRUDDH PRATAP SINGH
Assistant chief Instructor
(MITTI SYSTEM)

Mr. Aniruddh Pratap Singh
Commando Trainer

BRIGHT RAJPUT SPORTS LLP
Deals in Sports items

Mr. Daniel Joshua

Founder, Daniel's boomerang

[Maharajganj]

[Uttar Pradesh]

Dear mr. Daniel Joshua,

We at BR Sports are pleased to formally introduce ourselves as a dedicated manufacturer of premium cricket bats and sports equipment. It has been a privilege to collaborate with you and your esteemed brand, Daniel's Boomerang, as we work together to deliver quality products to sports enthusiasts around the world.

Our shared passion for excellence in sports innovation and equipment craftsmanship is the foundation of this partnership, and we are excited about the potential it holds. BR Sports remains committed to maintaining the highest standards in product quality and service, ensuring that both our brands continue to grow and earn trust across markets.

We also want to appreciate the consistency and dedication of the Daniel's Boomerang team in actively promoting the Boomerang brand and helping players gain visibility in Boomerang form. Their efforts have significantly contributed to building a strong presence in the cricketing community. We are equally excited to share that Boomerang products will soon be available at our BR Sports store, further strengthening our collaboration and reach.

We look forward to expanding this collaboration and exploring further opportunities that bring mutual success.

Thank you for your continued support and partnership.

Warm regards,

[B.R SPORTS]

[ANUJ CHAUHAN (CEO)]

For BRIGHT RAJPUT SPORTS LLP

H. No. 321, G/F, Chauhan Mohalla, Madanpur Khadar, New Delhi - 110076
Mob.:7838117373, 8587844261

Mr. Anuj Chauhan
CEO - B.R Sports

In a unique celebration of the boomerang sport, I wrote, composed, and recorded "The Boomerang Song". This upbeat anthem brings together throwers, boomsmiths, and enthusiasts from around the world, showcasing the sport's global reach and community.

The song delves into the world of competitive boomerang, highlighting various rounds and rules, while also exploring the sport's connection to history, arts, culture, and fitness.

I was honored to have Mr. Logan Broadbent, President of the International Federation of Boomerang Associations, participate in the music video and launch the song online. This special collaboration underscores the song's significance within the boomerang community.

"The Boomerang Song" is more than just a tribute – it's a testament to the power of music and sport to unite people across cultures and borders.
The song is available on all major platforms like Spotify, iTunes, Saavn, etc.

Watch the music video and experience the spirit of the boomerang community, Scan QR to listen.

The Boomerang Association of India

Forged in Passion. Backed by Purpose. Driven by Unity.

Every great movement begins with a vision. Ours was born in 2022, when a handful of passionate boomerang enthusiasts from across India began asking a simple yet powerful question:

"What if we had a national body—fair, inclusive, and built to truly uplift the sport in India?"

It wasn't just an idea—it was a calling. We knew we needed something that would represent throwers from every corner of the country, promote the sport with integrity, and set a high standard for boomerang culture in India.

But we also knew this couldn't be rushed. So, we gave it time. For three solid years, we worked in our own spaces—organizing workshops, hosting public demos, conducting training camps, experimenting with new designs, and planting the seeds of awareness wherever we could.

Not only we organized tournaments but also took part in them including virtual tournaments (World Boomerang League by Boompop) during this period—staying connected with the global community while building skills, momentum, and visibility back home.

We trusted the process, knowing that anything grown with care and patience will eventually bear good fruit.

And now, in 2025, that fruit has arrived.

We are proud to announce the official formation of the **Boomerang Association of India (BAI)**—a landmark initiative that unites India's finest boomerang throwers and creators under one powerful banner.

This association is more than just a registered national body—it's a declaration.

A declaration that India is here, serious, and ready to lead in the world of boomerangs. It represents the coming together of talent, tradition, innovation, and purpose.

There are various clubs across the country that are now recognized by this national body—each playing a crucial role in the growth and vibrancy of the Indian boomerang movement. Some of these pioneering clubs include:

- Sudarshan Boomerangs (Karnataka)

Run by Prasanna Mishrikoti, known for his low-flight special boomerangs and technical precision that has redefined style and control in Indian boomerang design.

- Karma Boomerangs (Tamil Nadu)

Founded by Philip Sathyaraj, known for his high-performance composite MTAs and for being the best individual scorer from India in the World Boomerang Championship.

- Sunil's Boomerang World (Madhya Pradesh)

Created by Sunil Uikey, who has a strong presence in the tribal community of Madhya Pradesh. His club focuses on inclusive workshops and nurturing young local talent. Sunil is also a powerful left-handed thrower, making him a unique and valuable asset to the sport in India.

- **Gold Trophy Master Nilesh Boomerangs (Maharashtra)**

Founded by Nilesh Gangawane, a multi-sport master whose precision and versatility have brought accolades in boomerangs and beyond.

- **Chakra Boomerangs (Madattukkulam)**

Founded by Dinesh Kumar, a versatile boomerang maker whose creations played a pivotal role in my early boomerang practice.

- **Satzzz Boomerangs (Chennai)**

Founded by Satish D, one of the youngest and most promising boomerang throwers and makers in the country. India's second composite boomerang maker, a rising star in innovation and performance.

- **Daniel's Boomerang (Uttar Pradesh & North India)**

Led by myself, Daniel Joshua, focused on education, awareness, and storytelling through workshops, outreach, and this very book.

We are humbled and honored to share that the **Oscar Cuartas Boomerang Foundation (OCBF)** has extended its support and encouragement to the Boomerang Association of India. As one of the most respected organizations in the international boomerang community, their recognition means the world to us. It reaffirms that our efforts matter—not just in India, but globally.

This support inspires us to stay grounded in our values while also aiming high for international presence, representation, and respect.

Every movement needs a crew — and this one's got a stellar lineup of hearts, hands, and heads who believe in making boomerang accessible to everyone:

I, **Daniel Joshua – President**

Philip Sathyaraj – Vice President

Prasanna Mishrikoti – Secretary

Nilesh Gangawane – Joint Secretary

Sunil Uikey – Treasurer

Shishir R John, Gulshan Chauhan, and Jai Pratap Singh – Founder Members

The Boomerang Association of India is committed to:

- Organizing official district, state, national championships and public events
- Establishing training standards and coaching certifications
- Launching school and youth outreach programs
- Promoting self-made designs and cultural integration
- Building India's global presence in international competitions and forums

We are creating not just an organization, but a legacy. A platform that will empower the next generation of Indian boomerang enthusiasts to dream big, throw far, and return stronger.

So if you ever see a boomerang spinning in the Indian sky—know that it carries more than just aerodynamic precision. It carries a story, a vision, and a nationwide movement that's only just beginning to soar.

From the writer's pen

From a young age, I held a profound fascination for the tool wielded by Mowgli in the captivating tale of the 'Jungle Book'. The miraculous boomerang that returned to him with each throw was a source of awe and wonder. Little did I realize then that one day I would have the ability to craft my own boomerangs. It was in 2021 that my mother-in-law Mrs. Shiwali Peter introduced me to the sport, igniting a passion within me. Since that moment, I have encountered numerous individuals immersed in the world of boomerangs.

Among these individuals, two of my friends, Sunil Uikey from Madhya Pradesh and Philip Sathyaraj from Tamil Nadu, have played an exceptionally influential role in my journey. One patiently guided me through the concept of throwing my initial boomerangs, while the other inspired me to venture into the art of crafting these remarkable objects. Ever since, I have wholeheartedly committed myself to the exploration and ongoing learning within this captivating sport.

In my perception, boomerangs transcend being simply a sport; they are a manifestation of artistry. I am continuously astonished by the variety of designs and materials that can be employed to create boomerangs, each yielding distinct outcomes. Furthermore, the flight of a boomerang is a dynamic phenomenon that can be manipulated to perform an array of awe-inspiring tricks, relentlessly driving me to seek mastery of new techniques.

At the core of my ambitions lies the goal of promoting this sport and fostering its popularity within our country. I actively engage with local communities, organizations, and enthusiasts in order to raise awareness about boomerangs and the sheer joy of throwing them. In my pursuit of excellence, I have had the privilege of connecting with esteemed boomerang throwers and artisans from around the globe, perpetually striving to refine my skills.

As the proud creator of the 'Namaste' boomerang model, I am honored to have achieved the remarkable feat of being the first Indian to have an original boomerang model featured in 'ScottW Boomerang Files.' This groundbreaking achievement not only represents my personal dedication to the art of boomerang crafting but also serves as a testament to the rich tradition of cultural expression through innovative design. I am thrilled to have made history for India in the boomerang community and can't wait to inspire others with this significant milestone.

I take this opportunity to express my heartfelt gratitude to individuals who have contributed to my journey. Sir Kendall Davis, renowned for his exceptional designs, the late Sir Hendricks Dave, with his invaluable tips and suggestions, Sir James Hoy, a mentor par excellence and Dr. Dara Cuartas for helping me organize my biggest events. I extend my heartfelt thanks to Sir Paul Bryden for graciously contributing his enlightening Brief-report on the history of boomerangs, which greatly enriched the content of this book.

I express my deepest gratitude to Sir Gary Broadbent for his exceptional dedication in proofreading this book and for generously imparting his invaluable expertise on boomerang profile and tuning whenever I needed help. Special vote of thanks to Mr. Ritesh Pitts for being an amazing part of the team Daniel's Boomerang.

I also extend my sincere appreciation to Alejo Palacio, Michael Siems, Manuel Schütz, Jorge Rivera, Ronaldo Alperin, Eric Sch, and all the boomerang enthusiasts who have generously shared their insights, ideas, and inspiring videos. Special thanks go to Ma'am Catherine Matheson for her moral support and Mr. Rajan Safri for his tireless efforts in organizing tournaments, as well as Dr. Anita Benjamin, whose guidance has been instrumental in my growth. Big thanks to Sangeeta ma'am who not only assisted me with the boomerang workshops but also joined me on various occasions.

Lastly, I gratefully acknowledge the unwavering support of my brothers Abhishek, Michael, and Johnson, who make up team D.B.. and my devoted wife Lydia, whose unwavering encouragement allows me the time to immerse myself in this delightful pursuit.

With boundless enthusiasm, I eagerly anticipate the unfurling of my future journey with boomerangs.

What lies before me is only the opening chapter, and I am filled with anticipation as I envision the paths that lie ahead.

I extend my deepest gratitude to you for taking the time to delve into my story, share in my passion, and accompany me on this remarkable voyage with boomerangs.

Daniel Joshua

With my parent's blessings

Rev. Joshua J Bhagat

Mrs. Elizabeth J Bhagat